Praise

'As a former weight-loss programme consultant and "yo-yo dieter" myself, I would heartily recommend that anyone who has found themselves constantly being drawn into restrictive, whacky or downright dangerous weight-loss plans, should take a look at this book. You will find a whole new door opening for you: a door into a way of life you never dreamed was possible, where you are in control of your own body – and your own dress size!'
— **Angela Roth**, business coach for heart-led entrepreneurs, Succeed From The Start

'*The Mindset Diet* will allow you to work through your own lifestyle influences, dietary patterns and triggers to identify how you can overcome barriers and make lasting changes to the way you eat to allow for safe, natural weight loss. Caroline has put together activities that you can complete in your own time to address your own limiting beliefs, allowing for habits to change so you can free yourself from the cycle of dieting and weight gain. After reading, you can start to ignore the number on the scales and look forward to being comfortable with how you feel.'
— **Jennifer Williams**, nutritional therapist

'*The Mindset Diet* really resonated with me. As I read about changing mindsets, I found myself reflecting on my own relationship with food and successfully changing my own thinking about what and how I eat. If you're fed up with yo-yo dieting and want to improve your relationship with food, I highly recommend this book.'
— **Kylie Combellack**, primary school teacher

'This is a truly must-have book for anyone who is interested in the relationship between the mind and diet. *The Mindset Diet* includes practical guidance, self-coaching activities and highly relatable stories from Caroline's own journey, which make it an easy, engaging and enjoyable read. As NLP continues to become an increasingly powerful vehicle for personal transformation, Caroline has applied NLP tools to an important area of our health. Readers can look forward to understanding and knowing themselves in a deeper way.'
— **Kate McCartney**, NLP Master Trainer, Toby & Kate McCartney Ltd

'There's a lot of talk about mindset these days, but do we really understand what that means? *The Mindset Diet* helps you become aware of what your mind is doing in relation to food. As you complete the simple, relatable exercises and reflect on how you think about food, your relationship to and with food changes. Your mindset changes. And with that change comes so much more – it is transformational.'
— **Jane Aronovitch**, former writer/editor and movement maven, Studio Jane

CAROLINE TYRWHITT

THE
MINDSET
DIET

To Kate,
Wishing you small steps
to your success of a flourishing future
Caroline Tyrwhitt
xx

Escape the trap of yo-yo dieting and go from disillusioned dieter to empowered eater

R^ethink

First published in Great Britain in 2024
by Rethink Press (www.rethinkpress.com)

Cover images licensed by Ingram Image

Contents

Introduction

Confession: I am a recovering yo-yo dieter. In my teens, I had learned to 'go on a diet' to lose weight each time I put it on. Regularly. It never occurred to me to change how I was living.

In my forties, I was too busy and too stressed to keep going on a diet. I had little tolerance to starving myself anymore. Occasionally, out of exasperation with my weight gain, I would try a diet, lose some weight, and predictably put it straight back on again as soon as I returned to my old lifestyle and habits.

I had become increasingly disillusioned with dieting and didn't want to invest precious time and energy on depriving myself anymore, yet I wasn't happy in my body. I didn't like my photo being taken when

I was on holiday, nor what I looked like in the mirror, nor the clothes I was wearing to hide my weight gain. I was judgemental and critical towards myself, somehow feeling not good enough as I wasn't looking successful.

It wasn't an empowered decision I had made not to diet – it was avoidance. I thought I was faced with an either/or choice: that I had to either ignore my eating while I focused on my career or work less and go on holiday less to find time and space to diet and exercise.

It seems I shared this yo-yo dieting pattern with many women. It never occurred to me that instead of going on a diet, I could *change* my diet; that a diet is not a temporary state of affairs, but part of my lifestyle. No one ever talked to me about keeping weight off as a long-term change.

Until I started learning Neurolinguistic Programming (NLP), I never questioned this going-on-a-diet strategy. NLP made me realise I could take a completely different approach to weight loss; it helped me change my thinking about dieting. I discovered I could make small changes to my lifestyle that would make me feel better and lose weight without feeling deprived.

After researching and reading around the topic of dieting, looking at factors that affect our weight, weight loss and weight gain, and exploring other mindset tools, I decided to use my experience to help women to shift their thinking about going on a diet. I created *The Mindset Diet* and now I'm sharing it with you.

What is NLP?

NLP is an attitude, a mindset, a set of tools and concepts. It helped me change my thinking. NLP sheds light on how we structure our experiences, our beliefs, our language, our behaviours, and helps us get different outcomes. It helps us understand how we are all unique, which is why one solution *doesn't* fit us all.

NLP works with both the conscious and unconscious mind. It provides tools and techniques to bring both your minds into alignment so that they share the same intention. When that happens, you will be more successful in your goals.

There are more NLP tools that could help you change your relationship with food than I have included in the book as they need an expert practitioner. For example, Timeline Technique, N-Step Reframe or Submodality Belief Change can shift limiting beliefs very quickly. Other tools such as Like to Dislike and Swish, which I have included, may be easier to use and more powerful when done with a practitioner.

How I have structured the book

There are four steps to learning. I have broken the book into four parts to reflect these steps and help you learn and adopt new ways of thinking so that you can easily change your relationship with food and stop going on a diet.

STEP FOUR
UNCONSCIOUS COMPETENCE
You've created a new set of beliefs, thoughts and behaviours you do naturally, occasionally readjusting should old habits creep back in.

STEP ONE
UNCONSCIOUS INCOMPETENCE
You don't know what you don't know — you have no awareness of how your environment and your habits are keeping you stuck in yo-yo dieting.

STEP THREE
CONSCIOUS COMPETENCE
You've made some fundamental changes, you're focused and clear on your goal. You build new habits to support your goal.

STEP TWO
CONSCIOUS INCOMPETENCE
You learn how your beliefs, values and thoughts drive your behaviours and start to unpick them and change some.

Four steps to learning

In Part One of the book, I guide you through the place to start any desired change, which is to observe yourself, your habits and how you do them. You can't change what you don't know, so I ask you to notice what unconscious behaviours, which in NLP are called your strategies, are driving your outcomes. When you make your habits conscious, you have more choice and you can choose to change them. I ask that you enjoy this in a curious and non-judgemental way.

In Part Two, you will learn how your inner landscape works and realise just how much goes on in your unconscious. You get the chance to declutter the thoughts, values and beliefs that underpin your present eating habits, which will give you more clarity. In NLP, we believe it is our inner landscape – these thoughts, values and beliefs – that affects how we react to any given event, and whether we succeed at change. After decluttering, you will begin to create more empowering versions for yourself.

Once you understand how your mind impacts your eating habits, it's time to create a well-formed outcome, a goal. I have left setting your goal until Part Three, because I want you to make a fundamental shift in how you think and see your relationship with food before you create your vision for yourself. Because your goal should be about more than weight loss. It is a chance to design your future.

As our unconscious mind is outcome oriented, NLP considers creating conscious, well-formed outcomes key to achieving what we desire. When you set a clear goal, you help your unconscious mind to filter your thinking towards that desired outcome and to pay attention to the opportunities and choices with which you are presented along the way. Part Three is also about building basic wellbeing habits that will help you achieve your goal.

In Part Four, we examine aspects of your environment and eating habits that can either support or sabotage your goal. I share strategies to make your eating more conscious, information to change your programmed attitude towards foods and what science tells us all about losing and gaining weight. This section also reflects my experience over several years after I stopped dieting. We'll explore both real and perceived barriers to achieving and maintaining your new lifestyle.

You can read *The Mindset Diet* in any order and try any combination of strategies, dip in and out, and utilise tools that feel right for you. I can't promise it will be comfortable reading, but it will help you to get off the yo-yo dieting rollercoaster.

I would suggest, though, that you start at the beginning so that you can understand how you got to this place of disillusionment. When you know what got you here, you can work out what will get you where you want to go and change more with every chapter. Read it through once, then flip back to what resonates most and the strategies you want to try. No one tool alone will be the miracle that will make it easier to lose weight and keep it off; it is a cumulative process.

Buy yourself a journal to work through the self-coaching activities so that you can really apply *The Mindset Diet* approach. Alternatively, you can download my bespoke workbook by visiting http://workbook.themindsetdietbook.co.uk/home or scanning the QR code at the back of the book. Reading this book will build your awareness, but it's only when you *apply* the knowledge that you will make meaningful change in your relationship with food.

The person with the greatest influence on you is you. Accessing your inner knowledge will give you wisdom and understanding to implement change. It will reveal the key to the sustainable lifestyle that is perfect for you. When you recognise that it will take a change in your eating habits and your lifestyle to have the body and energy you want, applying *The Mindset Diet* will give you tools to get there with more grace and ease and less self-judgement. After you've read the book, you'll end up making changes that impact on your confidence and impetus in business too.

Start making small changes right now. That's easy to do. You don't need to wait until you've lost weight to be an empowered eater.

PART ONE
OBSERVE

How do you know what to change if you don't know precisely what's going on in the first place? It makes sense to stand back and observe yourself before you start.

To reach our desired outcome of being an empowered eater, we start by observing how our environment contributes to yo-yo dieting, how we become disillusioned dieters, how we end up feeling like victims or failures. In this section of the book, we will look at all of this.

First, we'll explore how the diet industry operates and what scientists know about losing weight. Once you are more aware of how the system works to keep you in a yo-yo cycle, you will have more choices of what you can do to change.

Then, I'll guide you through observing your own eating habits and triggers and show you how you got stuck in the yo-yo dieting trap. Here, you will learn how you 'do' food, what your patterns are.

ONE

It's Not Your Fault – Diets Don't Work

Do you blame yourself each time you put back on the weight you lost through traditional or fad dieting? In this chapter, I shine a light on how we have become victims to an industry designed to keep us repeating behaviours that are giving us bodies we don't want and actually harming our wellbeing.

If we listen to our intuition, we're all likely to know deep down that dieting doesn't work. Yet we're so programmed with the go-on-a-diet thinking paradigm, we are afraid not to do so. When our body feels out of control, we desperately try the latest dieting fad, only to end up with the same results.

I'll show you how you have come to this place of not trusting your own judgement and give you an alternative way of thinking about your relationship with food. Then you can stop going on a diet.

The worth of the diet industry

According to Allied Market Research, the weight loss and weight management diet market was valued at US$192.2 billion in 2019, and is projected to reach US$295.3 billion by 2027.[1] Prescription weight-loss medications are a further multimillion-dollar market all on their own. Demand has soared for the diabetes injection used for weight loss and nicknamed 'the skinny jab', a solution that is only effective while you're using it, yet the industry is predicted to reach US$13.26 billion by 2029.[2]

Shouldn't the mere fact there are so many diets and weight-loss solutions out there with such a huge market value lead us to question just how effective they are?

A quick search on the internet gives us some interesting statistics from a woman's point of view around dieting. She:

- Spends between six and thirty-one years, or on average seventeen years, of her life on a diet[3]

- Invests as much as £20–25,000 over her lifetime on weight loss, including monthly memberships, special 'fat-free' or 'lo-cal' foods, supplements and meal plans, recipe books and magazines, gym memberships and new clothes[4]

- Tries as many as 126 diets in her lifetime – that's two or more diets a year[5]

- Loses her body weight nine times over[6]

- Gives up on her diet after an average of five weeks, two days and forty-three minutes[7]

Each year, 57% of women in the UK will try to lose weight and 64% say they're trying to lose weight most of the time.[8] This was borne out in a survey of my Facebook group, where most responders reported they diet on and off throughout the year and put the weight back on within a few months, or a year at most. They've tried a whole range of diet solutions, mostly weight-loss clubs, since they were in their teens or twenties.

Logically, we know dieting doesn't work because so many people repeatedly go on a diet. We may manage to lose weight, but then we put it back on again, in many cases more than we lost.

In 2022, 59% of women were overweight or obese in the UK, with those in the forty-five to seventy-four age groups most likely to be overweight.[9] I doubt that's from lack of dieting. In the United States, 69% of adults are either overweight or have obesity.[10] Globally, if these figures are unaddressed, an estimated 1 billion adults will have obesity by 2030.

Yet, still the supermarket shelves, high streets and TV advertising are dominated by food, while individuals are shamed and blamed for their weight, having bought in to the messages and given in to sales tactics. The UK's food and drink industry is now the country's biggest manufacturing sector by turnover, valued at £104.4 billion.[11]

The myths of dieting

The word 'fad' is frequently associated with diets, as is 'extreme' or 'crash'. Diets come and go in popularity, especially in this day of social media and celebrity offerings. They come with the promise of 'melting fat', 'dropping a dress size in a week' or losing weight 'effortlessly' or 'faster'. They may offer a miracle food or tell you about a new way to lose weight.

Most diets focus on a simplified approach of calorie reduction. The 'Twinkie Diet' showed how it's possible to lose weight on any diet, nutritious or not, if you significantly reduce your calorie intake. Dr Melinda Ratini at Web MD questions the extreme claims made by some diets, for example, losing 10 lb (4.5 kg) in three days. She calculates: 'To lose just 1 lb of body fat a week, you would need to reduce your daily calories by about 500 a day.'[12] She explains that this would mean giving up 3,500 calories over the course of seven days. 'If a diet makes a claim that you'll lose 10 lb in three days, it would require decreasing your calorie intake by 35,000 calories in that time.'

Experts generally believe that slow weight loss of about a pound a week is best.[13] Slow weight loss reduces body fat percentage and maintains resting metabolic rate.[14] This makes any weight loss more sustainable. Also, slower weight loss combined with resistance exercise has been shown to protect bone density, which is important for women.[15]

Fad diets are nothing new. 'The long, strange history of dieting fads', a report by Colorado State University, traces Beyoncé's Lemonade Diet back to 1941, while Lord Byron created the Apple Cider Diet in the 1820s.[16] This became fashionable in the 1950s and has been making the rounds again recently.

A widely quoted statistic is that 95% of people who lose weight put it back on within two years. However, this cannot be proven as it is not tracked. Companies who sell weight-loss products or services don't seem to keep a track of outcomes and even research studies find it hard to track participants over the long term. The *New York Times* reported:

> 'The limited data suggests that many people who complete commercial diets will regain one-third of their lost weight after one year, two-thirds or more after three years and most, if not all, in three to five years. And many will not even complete the program.'[17]

There has been some recent tracking of contestants on America's reality TV show *The World's Biggest Loser*, which found most put the weight they'd lost back on and some gained more than they lost.[18] Those who kept their weight gain to a minimum seemed to have incorporated what they'd learned into their daily life as a career, for example as a personal trainer or motivational speaker, which would require they stay focused on their eating choices.

It is not in the interests of diet companies to teach you how to keep weight off or to stop dieting as they rely on repeat and returning customers. Some healthcare professionals argue that the condition of obesity should be classed as a chronic disease rather than a lifestyle choice or treated as cosmetic, while others argue this would only benefit the pharmaceutical industry.[19] I would suggest that understanding how our eating is influenced gives us choices and empowers us to make change in a different way.

What you need to know before you start your next weight-loss journey

Your diet is not just the food you eat; it is how you spend your day, how you nourish your body and mind. It is socialising, friends and family, how you think and feel, your environment, the culture around you, and so much more.

Science is only just beginning to understand how the body regulates its weight. Our hormones drive our desire for food. A reduction in calorie intake leads to hormonal changes that stimulate appetite, reduce metabolic rate and increase the consumption of more calorific foods. Our genes also influence our weight: 85% of us carry so-called thrifty genes, which help us conserve energy and store fat during lean times.[20] Some people have a genetic predisposition to be overweight, with their genes accounting for an influence of anywhere from 25% to 80%.

Any diet works once, but the second time around you won't lose as much.[21] Furthermore, diets are not balanced, which means you may not get enough nutrition and could feel depleted of energy rather than feeling better. Research also suggests that 'dieting at one point in time is likely to predict weight gain at a later point in time',[22] as our bodies fight to put weight back on.[23] Another theory is we have a set point: our body has a weight range it wants to stay in and as we put on weight, our set point increases.[24] It is believed this is a key reason that people return to their pre-diet weight after doing a crash diet and that the only way to get it to decrease again is through slow weight loss.

Women typically have more body fat and less muscle than men, which affects the basal metabolic rate, or how many calories our body burns while at rest.[25] This means it takes women longer than men to lose the same amount of weight.

Focusing our attention on the subject of mindset, a foundation for much of the content of this book, let's look at ten reasons diets don't work for most people:

1. Dieting is a bit like taking a pill to help cure an ailment: it's just treating the symptoms and we can't wait for it to be over.

2. We keep thinking about what we can't have, which makes us feel deprived.

3. We have to follow the rules of the diet, and when we don't get them right, we feel frustrated, which often tempts us to give up.

4. Often, diets are too strict and radical, lacking flexibility. This makes them unsustainable, but we think they don't work because we're not good enough, that we have no willpower.

5. Our environment can subconsciously trigger the desire to eat without us realising it, which sabotages our plans.

6. We tend to be so programmed to multi-task that we eat while doing something else, or we eat quickly so we don't notice how much we're devouring or when we're full.

7. Diets don't teach us about nutrition, how our body works and how to create new sustainable eating habits, so we go back to our old eating habits again.

8. Diets don't look at how we got to be where we are right now and our triggers for overeating, so we may still eat in unhelpful ways.

9. Diets don't change our thinking – we still think as we did before, which is why we're at risk of putting all the weight we lost back on again.

10. We don't adapt our environment to maintain our new eating habits and lower weight, and so we gradually creep back to our old habits.

Now you have an understanding of how powerful the messaging is in our environment and the reasons why dieting doesn't work, you have a choice: you can continue to go on a diet, following traditional or fad approaches as we've all been conditioned to do, treating the symptoms, or you can try something different.

In the next chapter, I invite you to try a different approach. When you build your self-awareness around your eating triggers and patterns, you can start to understand how you are influenced by your environment and the habits you have formed. You can then make more empowered choices about your eating.

Summary

We have all become victims to an industry designed to keep us repeating behaviours that are giving us bodies we don't want and harming our wellbeing. This chapter has shown you how you have come to this place of not trusting your own judgement.

Quite simply, dieting doesn't work, because it only treats the symptom – being overweight, being unhappy with our body – not the underlying cause of our weight gain, and it doesn't consider how our bodies work. Just like taking a pill to cure an ailment, we can't wait for the diet to be over, and then we return to our old habits. Little wonder the weight goes back on again.

What we need is a change of mindset, a new way of thinking about diet, so it becomes a part of our lifestyle, not just a temporary fix. In the next chapter, we will look at what lies behind our eating habits.

TWO

Acknowledge Your Eating Habits

Have you ever wondered if there's more to losing weight than you've been taught, because nothing you try seems to work? Scientific understanding is growing in the field of our relationship with food, and we are beginning to find more ways to educate ourselves on how to eat to keep a healthy mind and body and understand why diets don't work.

Not only is losing weight a complex issue from a scientific point of view, but after years of fad diets, you are likely to have less energy and willpower to go without and stick to the rules. You are also likely to have lost your trust in your ability to know how to feed yourself.

In this chapter, I will show you how your eating habits are unconscious, how you have become trapped in yo-yo dieting and how your habits are linked to your environment and elements that make up your personality. Despite it being a mass industry, dieting is a personal affair and what works for one person doesn't work for someone else. Your relationship with food is unique to you and affects your success at dieting.

Understand yo-yo dieting

I'm sure you've heard of the term yo-yo dieting, but what exactly is it? It's the process of repeatedly going on a diet, switching between depriving yourself and losing weight, and giving up, going back to your former eating habits and putting the weight back on. This is so common that yo-yo dieting is the nickname given to what is more formally known as weight cycling.

From an emotional point of view, yo-yo dieting is when you find yourself choosing a drastic diet to get rid of your weight gain fast. It works at first, then it doesn't, so you give up. You feel unsuccessful, blame yourself. Desperate to get back control of your body and feel better, you try again, rarely succeeding and usually feeling more and more disillusioned each time around.

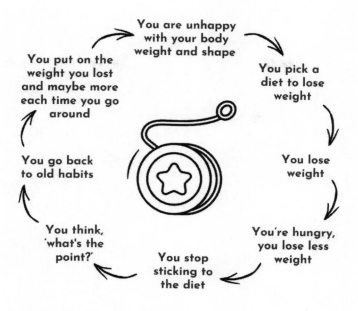

The yo-yo diet

From a scientific point of view, over-dieting slows your metabolism, yet your hunger doesn't decrease to match, which suggests that dieting won't work.[26] In addition, dieting can reduce your muscle mass and increase your body fat percentage, which is the opposite of what dieters set out to achieve.[27] This is one reason why most dieters regain the weight they lose and some become even heavier than when they started. Yet the blame for this failure seems to sit with us, the dieters; that it's we who yo-yo; that we know what we're doing and we're choosing this route.

You're stuck in negative thinking, triggered eating, and unhelpful habits. You dislike your body and don't prioritise self-care. You eat lots of refined carbs, sugars. You're scared to weigh yourself. You're in a state of powerlessness.

You feel sluggish/tired, but without negativity about yourself. You believe you're eating okay and don't understand why you feel like you're putting on weight. You have some treats.

You manically diet and exercise. You're focused and optimistic. You use words like 'must', 'should', 'need', 'have to'. You're adrenalin fuelled, but often exhausted and hungry so you get irritable. You weigh yourself daily. You feel in control.

You diet through careful choice of foods rather than obsessively following a diet's rules and you never diet for an extended period. You do some exercise to help you lose weight.

EXTREME

EXTREME

BALANCED

You think clearly, proactively. Your actions and emotions are balanced. You feel well. You practise self-compassion. You choose to eat nutritious foods all the time and some other foods occasionally. You listen to your body. You move regularly and have routines to look after your wellbeing.

Yo-yo pendulum model (adapted from a concept shown to me by psychotherapist and coach Linda Barbour)

Some of you may have found yourself swinging like a pendulum from obsessively dieting to feeling out of control, negligent or guilty when eating foods you 'shouldn't' eat, or eating too much because you've given up. If you have been inspired by a diet, rigidly followed that diet, got bored by it, broken its rules, and then told yourself you're rubbish at dieting, then you're probably on this pendulum, swinging from one side to the other. You may have lost touch with your body and the true reason to eat food, any food. Your relationship with food probably feels broken.

The reason you bounce from one extreme to the other is not because you're no good at dieting; it's because neither side is sustainable or healthy. Neither makes you feel truly well or brings you lasting happiness. You may even have learned as a result of the two extremes of the pendulum to resent food and doubt yourself.

Imagine stilling that pendulum in the middle. Imagine feeling balanced, in tune with your environment and food, in tune with you. If you let go of the notion of going on a diet and adopt instead the mindset of changing your diet, where diet in this context is your whole lifestyle, then you will find that balance. You will get rid of that feeling of being permanently deprived because you won't always be thinking you 'should' be on a diet or about what you 'can't' or 'shouldn't' have. When you choose to *nourish* yourself, you'll find that balance.

My Story

I've lost count of how many times I went round that yo-yo cycle. When younger, I spent time at the dieting extreme. More recently, though, I hovered just below as I fluctuated through the yo-yo cycle, finding moments of inspiration to diet, and then soothing my exhaustion and rewarding my hard work with treats. I would find my weight had slowly crept back on when I'd been too busy, stressed and tired to do anything, until suddenly I couldn't fit in an all-important outfit, or I was going on holiday and unhappy at having to bare my body for all to see.

Sometimes, when the January New Year's resolutions came around, I'd start a diet, but I had no real motivation so it never lasted long. Once, I joined a gym and wasted thousands of pounds never going after the first few visits. Mostly, I'd get bored with the diet or have so many upcoming events where I couldn't follow the rules, I'd give up.

As I got older, I lost less and less weight each time I went on a diet and became disheartened sooner. I'm sure you know that heart-sinking feeling when you have followed your diet exactly, you're expecting to have lost weight, but when you get on the scales, you see you haven't lost anything. Zilch. Nada. No reward for all that effort – so what's the point? Might as well give up!

I've been there, many times.

CASE STUDY: Debra's lightbulb moment

When I showed a client, Debra, the pendulum model, she immediately recognised that she had been on this all her life. In that moment, she realised just how tired she was of her struggle with food, with the emotional highs from losing weight to lows of self-sabotage and decided that she wanted to change. She was coming up to a significant birthday and was disillusioned that she was on the extreme end of disliking herself and being uncomfortable in her body at this moment in her life. She wanted to feel better and had no intention of yo-yoing into her next decade.

Working with me on other areas, which we will cover later in this book, areas that resonated with her, she found the right balance in the right way for her. This had a knock-on effect at home and in her business life. She became confident with her weight for the first time since she had been ten years old.

 SELF-COACHING ACTIVITY 1:
Yo-yo cycle reflection

Think about what we have just learned concerning yo-yo dieting, and then consider:

- Where are you in the cycle?
- Where do you sit on the pendulum?
- Describe your pattern and how it makes you feel.

A model for change

When you think about change, what is the first approach that comes to mind? I'm guessing it's to change what you *do*.

Robert Dilts, a leading developer in NLP, introduced a model based on the idea that we cannot make change at the level we're at, we must make it at a higher level.[28] He identified six levels at which we can effect change and arranged them in a pyramid called the Neurological Levels of Change model.

The fundamental level of change, the base of the pyramid, is our environment – the where, when and who. The next layer for change is our behaviour. Notice that most of the advice we hear about losing weight is around change on these two levels. On the level of environment, a traditional diet approach tells us to empty our cupboards of food that is 'forbidden' and join a slimming club to be with others on the same journey. On the level of behaviour, we're told to eat less, exercise more, eat low-calorie dessert bars, avoid fats or eat fewer carbs.

The Mindset Diet will give you skills and capabilities (Dilts's third level) to effect wider change. You may identify skills at this level, for example cooking or nutritional knowledge, that would empower you to make further change. We have already started to examine the effects of your environment on your

EXAMPLES

	WHAT THE LEVEL MEANS
Purpose	Your vision, legacy, your why
Identity	Your persona, how you show up, 'I am...'
Values/Beliefs	Assumptions, stories, what's important to you
Skills/Capability	Already have/could develop
Behaviour	What you do, how you react, your habits, routines
Environment	Where/when/who

Purpose
To feel light and supple and move with ease
To be a parent/grandparent with lots of energy

Identity
I'm a comfort eater   I'm just like my mum
I've always been this way   I'm lazy

Values/Beliefs
I have no willpower   I want to relax after work
Losing weight is difficult   Life's too short

Skills/Capability
Understand food labels   Cooking
Paddleboarding   Nutrition expert

Behaviour
Eat when bored   Wear black
Start over on Mondays   Sabotage

Environment
In the car   While watching TV
With friends   Late at night

Dilts's Neurological Levels of Change model

eating, and in this chapter we'll look in more depth and begin to study your behaviours.

Changes above the skills and capability level are the most powerful, and the core of this book will help you focus on shifting your beliefs and values, being clear on your identity and purpose to make change on the levels below easier.

You can use Dilts's model to identify what is getting in your way of achieving any goal by starting at the base level and working your way up, framing the explanations of each level on the right as questions to support your thinking. When you have got to the top and are clear on your purpose, work your way back down through the levels to identify anything that would be more helpful at each one.

Remember to be compassionate and non-judgemental with yourself about what you uncover using this tool. From an NLP perspective, people are *not* their behaviours, and every behaviour has a positive intention – even the worst. If you can identify that positive intent, you can create a new behaviour with the same intent and you won't need the old behaviour.

Understand triggered eating

Is there a food that the mere sight of it makes you desperate to eat it? Do you go to the supermarket to buy ingredients to make your dinner, only to be tempted by the foods stacked near the checkouts and end aisles, packaged in bright colours or labelled as special offers? Then you can't get them out of your mind, and you end up eating something you 'shouldn't'?

If you see an ad for food on the TV, do you feel hungry? Do you then go and get something to eat? You may have been focused and intentional with your eating all day, and suddenly you find yourself craving a calorie-filled meal because you walked past a fast-food outlet on your way home, saw a huge picture of a nice, juicy burger and you really can't resist.

Perhaps you have a pot of sweets on your desk. A packet of biscuits sitting by the kettle. Jelly beans in your car glove compartment. You can't help yourself but eat one or two, or three or four.

This is triggered hunger or triggered eating. In other words, we're triggered to want to eat – our body prepares to eat – by the mere sight or smell of food (real or otherwise), which makes us think we're hungry. We end up fighting our willpower, often giving in, and then we berate ourselves. Perhaps we even eat more than we intended to make it worthwhile.

One of the reasons for the obesity crisis in the modern world is the huge number of cues to eat that surround us all day. It's these that cause us to overeat. We no longer eat because we are hungry, but because we've run the gauntlet of fast-food shops and eventually caved in at the smell from one of the outlets.

Notice how many fast-food logos are red and/or yellow. That's because, as research has shown, those colours cause excitement in our brain and can trigger the desire to eat.[29] We also see it in supermarket signs and packaging. Further research has shown that working or living near fast-food restaurants increases our likelihood of obesity.[30]

When you start taking back control, it is helpful to notice how much of your eating is triggered rather than genuine hunger. Write down the triggers, including those you manage to ignore. Once you become aware and recognise triggered hunger, you can choose whether to eat that food or not. Eventually, the trigger will have less of an impact on you. Alternatively, you could change your environment to remove the trigger by, for example, taking a different route to work.

Audit your dieting and eating habits

Have you heard people say that we are the sum of our habits? This idea, first introduced millennia ago by Greek philosopher Aristotle, suggests to me that how we 'do' food defines our future. If we want a different outcome, then first, we need to know our habits.

No one else has the same habits as you. Most of them are invisible as you predominantly live on autopilot. It takes courage to shine a light on yourself, but if you embrace the art of reflecting on the habits you have accumulated over the years, you will get a different outcome.

This is not a quick fix, but it is a powerful strategy for change. When you consider how much energy you have put into losing weight over the years, investing in a week of research seems a tiny sacrifice in comparison, and it will serve you well.

If you need further convincing, think how much money you've spent dieting, on for example:

- Diet foods
- Diet books
- Diet programmes
- Diet pills
- Gym memberships that remain unused
- New clothes each time you change a dress size
- Medication for weight-related health conditions

How much time have you wasted on dieting? How many:

- Months a year?
- Years since you did your first diet?
- Cold winter evenings going to weigh-ins?

- Hours thinking you must, should or need to go on a diet?

- Hours complaining about how rubbish you are at dieting?

- Hours feeling guilty about what you've eaten?

- Hours searching on the internet for a weight-loss miracle?

What about your opportunity cost? What:

- Don't you do because you're on a diet?

- Don't you do because you haven't lost weight yet?

- Can't you do because of your weight or health?

- Inspiring New Year's resolutions have you ignored to focus on losing weight?

- Jobs or clients have you missed out on because other people have judged you on your weight?

When you add all that up, surely it's worth taking the time to understand how you've got to where you are now so you can change to sustain the body you want. That's an empowered life.

You may know immediately what some of your habits are. To uncover others, you may want to observe yourself and take notes for a week. This should be a non-judgemental process; it is not about blaming and shaming yourself, but about research so that you get those lightbulb moments and start to understand yourself. When you track the behaviours you've learned, the triggers that set you off, you can change the habits and patterns you're unaware you've been busy building.

There are some common patterns that many of us have. Perhaps you're overwhelmed at work, too busy to eat what and when you need to, and too tired to prepare a healthy meal when you get home, so you grab a bite on the run, eat while you're working, 'inhale' whatever is available. Often, you don't even enjoy it.

Perhaps you're in a permanent cycle of stress and exhaustion. You wake up tired and hungry and choose foods that will give you a quick energy boost. Then, you spend the day managing your cravings for sugar, looking for something small and sweet to snack on. You feel like you have no willpower.

Perhaps you eat to feel better or to reward yourself for having got through yet another traumatic day. You plonk yourself down on the sofa with your diet meal, thinking that you deserve something better. Diet goes out of the window.

Perhaps you regularly go on a diet, lose your weight, and then overeat again when something goes wrong in your life. You feed your disappointment, and before you know it, you're back in your big clothes, wondering what happened.

When you recognise your patterns, you can start to identify your triggers so you can interrupt each pattern and create a new one. If it's the right pattern for you, it will feel light and easy, and your confidence will grow each week. You won't have to fight your willpower. The more you practise your new habits, the more they will become your autopilot, programmed into your unconscious mind.

 SELF-COACHING ACTIVITY 2:
Your diet habits

Create a list of all the things you do to lose weight. Divide them into three columns – successful, unsuccessful or make no difference.

With a highlighter, mark up those that are easy for you and that you enjoy. Keep those. They are your successful habits.

Look at the rest and decide whether you would rather ditch or reframe each one. Ask yourself what about each habit doesn't work, what does work and what you could change about it.

 SELF-COACHING ACTIVITY 3:
Your eating habit diary

1. Keep an eating habit diary for one week. Unlike diaries you may have kept before to count calories, this diary will focus on your patterns, triggers and enjoyment.
I want you to track what you eat, but also when you eat, where you eat, who you eat with, why you have chosen to eat at that moment, how long you spend eating, how

much you eat, how full you are afterwards. Be curious and observe – eg, note whether you're stressed after a difficult conversation, tired and have no energy to cook, whether you saw... or smelled... or thought... Then rate how much you enjoyed what you ate. I also recommend you track your sleep and your movement.

Remember, no judgement.

Do this to track your normal days. It's not about being good or bad, but about uncovering what is really going on for you with food, what happens when. You can only change your patterns if you know what they are in the first place.

2. Go through your diary with a highlighter and look for patterns. Highlight in green all the things that went well. Highlight in amber opportunities to create change. Think about your triggers and how you could remove them and stop your old habits playing out. Think about new habits you could introduce. One small change at a time.

3. As you read this book, come back to the list and reconsider. What else could you change and where could you make more empowered choices?

My story

When I did my own eating diary, I realised that every day, I would be so tired and busy, I'd stop at the petrol station on the way to and from work to buy a coffee. I would then decide to buy a muffin or flapjack to go with it. Normally, I drink an Americano, but they take so long to cool down, I chose cappuccino instead – even more unhealthy fats, sugars and calories.

My response was to buy a good-quality refillable coffee cup so I could make an Americano before I left home and work. I'd not go in the petrol station, so I'd not buy and eat the cake either. This was a key strategy to change my eating habits. In fact, shortly after that, I started preparing a breakfast of berries and chia to take with me and kept nuts and seeds in the car for the evening. I have maintained this habit for years now.

CASE STUDY: TT's eating diary ahas

TT had quite a few aha moments when she did her eating diary. She realised she ate some foods that she thought were treats out of habit, but when she analysed it, she hadn't actually enjoyed them when she had eaten them. It was triggered or mindless eating. The next week, she chose to eat more consciously and only select foods she knew she would enjoy.

She noted that she mostly ate while doing something else, particularly watching TV, which meant she hadn't enjoyed what she had eaten and didn't feel full. She decided to interrupt this pattern by sitting somewhere else to eat, for example at the table.

TT noticed her sleep was interrupted because she got up to eat after she had gone to bed. This was because she had created a belief: 'I know if I eat, I will sleep'. In our sessions, we were able to break this habit down to find its root cause and create a new sleep routine that was designed to interrupt her old habit. Once her unhelpful bedtime routine was interrupted, not only did she eat less at night and sleep soundly, but she was less hungry the following day.

Summary

Dieting is a personal affair and what works for one individual doesn't work for someone else. In this chapter, we looked at letting go of the notion of going on a diet and adopting instead the mindset of changing our lifestyle.

When we start taking back control, it is helpful to notice how much of our eating is triggered rather than genuine hunger. Once we become aware and recognise triggered hunger, we can choose to eat that food or not. When we track the behaviours we've learned, the triggers that set us off, we can change those habits.

The Mindset Diet is about developing new thinking patterns that empower us to make eating decisions that are right for us rather than desperately following yet another set of dieting rules. In this chapter, we have looked more deeply into how our environment affects our thinking and our beliefs about food. If you're ready to escape the frustrating mind games and set yourself on the road to food freedom, then it's time for the inner declutter in Part Two.

The next part of the book is all about uncovering what got you to where you are and what will work to get you out of here. It is about looking deeper at your patterns, your habits, your strategies. Because once you know how you approach your relationship with food, blame-free, you can start to make the best changes for you, one small step at a time.

PART TWO
DECLUTTER

Don't you love a good declutter? Clutter prevents us from having a clear vision. It affects our mood and self-esteem. Having a clear-out is cathartic, giving us insights, a sense of relief, an opportunity to let go of the past and a chance to start over. Clearing the kitchen cupboards of foods that don't feature in the lifestyle we desire, putting away the clothes that don't fit us yet and giving away those that are now too big will focus our unconscious mind and set us up for success to change our diet.

Decluttering the thoughts, values and beliefs that are affecting your eating habits is fundamental to your success. It is your inner landscape, those thoughts, values and beliefs, that affects how you react to any given event. It is your inner landscape that determines your decisions and influences whether you succeed at change, whether you achieve your dreams. In Part Two, we examine the inner landscape that has got you to where you are now and is holding you back from being the woman you want to be. This part is about reframing and taking responsibility for what you can change.

Aristotle said, 'Give me a child until he is seven and I will show you the man.' In NLP, we work from the concept that the beliefs that hold us back and propel us forward are formed during the years of one to seven, and as adults, we can relearn those unhelpful beliefs we formed as we grew up. Effectively, our inner child will rule and run our adult life in an unhelpful way unless we update those values and beliefs that we formed in our early years.

In the chapters of Part Two, you will start to identify the narratives and beliefs that underpin your behaviours and where they came from. You will unravel where they are outdated so that you can alter them to match your adult persona and change your relationship with food.

THREE

Unravel Your Relationship With Food

How often have you promised yourself that you will get fit and lose weight? However, within a short time, you start to struggle to keep going, you run out of willpower. Either that, or you never quite find the perfect time to start.

Working on your mindset will support you to become the new woman you wish to be. When you start unravelling you, you can create change at a deeper level. You will no longer have to wrestle with your willpower, because you will have considered the inner workings – the beliefs and values you may not even be aware are driving your behaviours.

If you feel trapped in your behaviour choices, this chapter will help you explore what is keeping you stuck. It will give you tools to change your unhelpful beliefs and values, that all-important higher tier in Dilts's Neurological Levels of Change, and create more empowering beliefs – beliefs that will inspire and motivate you to be the best version of yourself.

Write your food story

We all have a food story, and writing yours down will help you identify the beliefs you have created over time and the values you had instilled in you as a child that have led to the eating habits you have as an adult. You learned these as you observed, listened to and absorbed the attitudes of those around you, as well as being affected by significant events.

Sadly, food is used as a control tool by both children, who will or won't eat what they're served, and adults, who are either flexible or inflexible in their attitudes to what must, should or needs to be eaten. Your story may illuminate your 'right' and 'wrong' foods, why you may use food to show love or as a reward, or how it may be functional for you. Through your story, you may understand why eating is a secret or a community affair for you, why you prepare meals with passion or consider it to be a chore.

As a child, you may have learned to cook meals as cheaply as possible or to splash out at restaurants. Exercise or activity may have been central to your life or perhaps they were something you avoided. Your story will identify how you learned to diet: if dieting was something you read about, learned at home or absorbed from the media around you. You may remember conversations about body types and genes to explain away your body shape.

My story

Food was a control issue from a young age for me as I had to eat a vegetarian diet: my dad's life choice was to be a vegetarian, a value inherited from his father. That meant foods were associated with being good or bad, allowed or not allowed. It also created secretive eating behaviours and eating for the sake of it when I went to visit friends, as I was encouraged to try what they were eating on the promise they 'wouldn't tell my dad'.

On the other hand, I was blessed with a diet of fresh vegetables grown in the garden by my dad, and home-baked bread and cakes along with a never-ending supply of preserves that my mum made. Dinner was family time – we always ate together in the evening at the kitchen table, and we all had to contribute to the cooking. I also learned to read food labels early on – to make sure there were no animal fats in the product.

When I was about ten years old, I remember being upset because my doctor told me to go on a diet, yet I know now I was probably carrying puppy fat. Not only did we eat a healthy diet, but I had the same netball skirt all the way through secondary school – it just got shorter!

My grandmother would make comments on female passers-by, friends and family, especially my mum, and

---

my father learned this right to comment on someone's appearance. I learned from this that women's bodies were clearly a matter for opinion and public discussion.

I grew up believing it was not OK to be fat. My dad has always been very slender, as has my brother most of his life, and my grandmother was slender even in her eighties.

I was a size 10 and 5 foot 6 inches at the age of fourteen to fifteen, which was probably average. I recall being right on fashion, pouring myself into tight jeans and lying on the bed to do them up with a hanger, desperate to be skinny. No forgiving Lycra in those days! My mum has great legs and arms and has always been slender, except her stomach. Having been put in corsets as a teenager, she'd never developed strong tummy muscles and when she had a baby, it stretched them and she couldn't get them to go back.

From a young age, I saw my mum dieting and, as a teenager, I joined her. I believed that dieting was normal, that it was what women did. My mum and I would often eat different foods to my dad and brother – we were on a diet! For example, on a Friday night, they would have fried egg, chips and beans, and we would have poached egg, cottage cheese and raw mushroom. Then we went back to eating 'normally' – until the next time. I could probably have got a qualification in calorie counting.

I was taught to eat everything on my plate. Regularly, I heard the phrase familiar to so many of us in the West that 'Kids are dying of starvation in Africa' or 'There are people who would be grateful for what you've been given', along with 'Waste not, want not' and 'I've slaved for hours to get the meal on the table', so I learned you don't stop eating when you're full, but when the plate is empty. I even learned to eat foods I don't like so there was no waste.

That is fine when you have a small dinner plate of good-quality home-cooked food and lots of vegetables, which I grew up with, but not so good when it's a giant pasta bowl of spaghetti bolognese, loaded with cheese and accompanied with garlic bread, and ne'er a vegetable in sight.

As a young adult, I developed the narrative of not having time to cook, which affected my eating choices. For example, I'd buy easy-fix foods that were starting to appear in the supermarkets at the time, stop to buy food on the way home from work or a night out, and choose to eat out several times a week. I slid away from the values of home cooking and home baking I had grown up with, influenced by the changes in the food industry and on our high streets. That temporary fix of dieting blossomed into its full power each time I noticed I'd put on weight in my twenties.

In my thirties, I started teaching, quit smoking and moved in with my partner. At this point, several things in my life collided. I lost cigarettes as an appetite suppressant. My partner uses food as a reward, especially desserts, which I started eating as an alternative to a cigarette. We also bought a new set of dishes that included the huge pasta bowls I mentioned; what I didn't know at the time was that my partner likes eating out of a bowl, and he would fill it.

I was ambitious to progress in teaching and worked long hours to make sure I got everything perfect. The time-poor narrative kicked in again. I was often exhausted,

> so I ate out regularly or bought luxury ready meals as a
> treat. Along with eating everything that I was given at
> home in those bowls, because I didn't want to appear
> ungrateful, I learned to eat a luxury dessert most days
> and developed the habit of drinking wine each night to
> relax as I worked on endless teacher admin, and to
> reward myself for my hard work. I put on weight, but
> I had less and less time or energy to go on a diet.
> Tomorrow thinking kicked in.

SELF-COACHING ACTIVITY 4:
Attitude to food

Now you have read my story with regards to the
attitudes to food I developed when young, it's time to
consider yours. Here are a few questions that you can
ask yourself. When you were growing up:

- What was the attitude to food in your home?
- What were the habits and atmosphere around
  eating times?
- What was the attitude to cooking, food shopping
  and preparation?
- What is your earliest memory of food?
- What rules were there in your house about eating?
- What messages were passed down to you about
  food and body shape?
- How did your parents talk about food?
- Did you have the same or different food to your
  peers or others in your household?

SELF-COACHING ACTIVITY 5:
Your food story

Now it's time to start writing *your* food story to see what early influences there were on your beliefs and your attitude towards food and physical activity. As you write, don't judge yourself, edit or censor your writing. Just allow your thoughts to flow unfettered.

This is a critical piece of inner work so that you can see where your eating behaviours have come from. We all have lots of beliefs about food and dieting, and when you identify yours, you can get to the root of your relationship with food. If you want to change that relationship, you will be more successful if you know what got you to where you are now.

What you believe, you achieve

Have you seen the lovely meme attributed to Oprah Winfrey that tells us we become what we believe rather than what we want? Yet even she did not make the connection between her beliefs and her weight until recently. Since reading Eckhart Tolle's *The Power of Now*,[31] she has focused on her inner self. On her website, she says, 'Because what you give your attention to looms larger – in this case literally – all my focus on weight actually made me fatter. Wasted time.'[32]

If you obsess about your weight and dieting, yet doubt your ability to lose weight; if you are increasingly disillusioned with dieting, yet rigidly follow dieting rules; if you're sick of trying to eat less and exercise more, it's time to dig deeper and focus on you, not your weight. It's time to do the uncomfortable inner work, because that is where growth and change happen. When your thoughts, values, beliefs and identity match where you want to go, you will get there.

When we look at the top tiers of Dilts's Neurological Levels of Change, we see that beliefs are key drivers for making lasting change. By changing the belief that you should go on a diet, a temporary behaviour, to the belief that you would be better served by changing your diet, a long-term holistic solution, you will alter your relationship with food forever.

Beliefs are thoughts we have over and over. They're the stories we tell ourselves and they are what we filter everything we experience through. It's like we have a filing cabinet – our unconscious mind – and our thoughts are there in the background all the time. Sometimes, they are invisible to us. Because we are so used to them, we fail to notice them anymore, yet they are impacting the choices we make. It is our unconscious thinking that affects our decision making and creates our habits.

Most of what we do all day is guided by our unconscious mind. According to neuroscientists, only 5% of our decisions, actions, emotions and behaviour choices are done consciously.[33] The remaining 95% are driven by our unconscious. Our brain can't consciously process the many gigabytes of information we are subjected to daily, so it has filters that we have programmed over time to sift it through:

- Memories, which were formed according to our perspective at the time

- Language – the words we use and recognise, and their connotations

- Beliefs and attitudes – our opinion of us and the world around us

- Strategies – how we know to do what we do, like breathe, walk, eat, clean our teeth, drive a car

Our programming creates our individual map of the world and it affects how we think and feel and behave in response to any given event or experience. We all have our own map that is unlike anyone else's as we all have unique experiences. It's why our food story governs our eating habits. It's why my idea of a perfect lifestyle may be different to yours.

When you see the evidence to support a belief, it fires the neurons in your brain and reinforces that belief. The more you experience it, the stronger the connection. For example, if you watched your mum diet over and over, missing out and starving herself only to put the weight back on, and each time you've tried to diet you've experienced the same, you probably believe that weight loss is difficult.

Beliefs can be empowering or limiting. We all have the potential to do something and take action that produces results. The action we take, the results we get and our perception of those results determine our belief about how easy or difficult something is.

An empowering belief frees us to reach our potential. The stronger our belief that we can, the more action we take, and the more results we will get. Limiting beliefs are stories we tell ourselves about what we can't do and what is wrong with us, and they keep us in a box. They keep us stuck, going around in circles, and can even sabotage us when we're successful.

If you operate from a limiting belief that dieting's difficult, you will struggle to access your potential, your actions will be of a lower quality and you'll have less determination, and of course, the results you get will be inferior, which then reinforces the belief that you can't lose weight and it all becomes a self-fulfilling prophecy – 'I was right!' A belief that you're not good enough can also cause self-sabotage when you've lost weight as you're not able to maintain the feel-good factor that comes with your success, or you don't believe you deserve it.

You can easily identify a limiting belief: when evidence is produced to contradict it, you respond with 'yeah, but' followed by why you can't do something or don't have something. Words and phrases that indicate you have a limiting belief at play are 'always', 'never', 'should', 'must', 'I keep on', and excuses that come with the word 'because'.

You can change a belief, though, because it is just that – a belief. It is not fact. You may believe you can't help how you are or that you can't change, but that's not true. By choosing a new belief, you allow yourself to be more flexible in your thinking and self-regulation.

Given your brain creates about 700 new neurons a day,[34] you can use this process to create thought and belief patterns. Our filters ignore anything that contradicts our beliefs, so you have to consciously look for evidence to support your new belief.

You can begin reshaping your beliefs simply by challenging the negative thoughts that get in your way, batting them away and repeating the belief you want to hold instead. An empowering response is kind and compassionate and focuses you on what you want.

Let me give you some examples:

I can't lose weight easily like other people can	I will lose weight as slowly or as quickly as is right for me and my mind and body allow
I'm not very attractive anyway	I have a beautiful smile that lights up my eyes when I feel proud and strong
I love food too much to diet	I love life and food that gives me energy to live my best life

Identifying where your thoughts and beliefs come from and what you could let go of to allow yourself to be your best you is an empowering experience. It's like an onion – you pull back one layer, work on it, and then later, you discover another layer. It's a continuous process that becomes easier the more you do it.

 SELF-COACHING ACTIVITY 6:
Identify your beliefs

Mark the beliefs in the list below that really resonate with you and write down any others that you may have about dieting and your relationship with food. Write down beliefs that hold you back from eating in a way that is helpful to you having the body you want. For example:

- I don't deserve to lose weight.
- My metabolism is slow.
- It's hard to lose weight now I'm older.
- I'm big boned.
- I can't lose weight no matter what I try.
- I've always been fat.
- Being fat is in my genes.
- My mum fed us rubbish so I don't know how to eat.
- I'm too lazy.
- I don't have time to diet.
- It's too expensive to eat healthily.
- I'm useless at exercising.
- I'm too unfit to exercise.

- I'm rubbish at cooking.
- I enjoy all the wrong foods.
- I hate vegetables.
- I've got a sweet tooth.
- I can't control my eating.
- I've got no willpower.
- I give in to what everyone else wants.
- I can't be bothered to eat different foods to everyone else.

Uncover some other beliefs that may be sabotaging you by finishing these sentences:

- I should look...
- I must be...
- I need to feel...
- Thin people are...
- Fit people are...
- When I am overweight, people think...
- Overweight people are not likely to...
- Losing weight is important because...

SELF-COACHING ACTIVITY 7:
Rewrite a belief

Choose a belief, and then write a more helpful version, like the examples in the table we looked at earlier. What if you decide that the new belief is true? It is only you who has decided the opposite was true in the first place. It is a belief you have created.

To help embed the new helpful belief:

- Write down all the evidence that you already have to support that new belief – *all* of your evidence. Don't question it, don't doubt it, don't write it off.

- Create a poster or some form of visual stimulation in your environment that you will see every day to remind yourself of this new belief.

- Look for yet more evidence that this new belief is true over the next month and keep adding the evidence to your list.

- Decide to accept that this new belief is true and start rewriting your story.

CASE STUDY: Debra shifts a limiting belief

Debra held the belief 'I am disorganised'. This came up as she reflected on not liking to-do lists and how this affected her relationship with her husband, who loved lists. When Debra realised this belief was untrue, as she was meticulously organised in her business, she gave herself permission to change the belief and allow herself to be organised everywhere. We used a hypnotherapy technique to help with this.

As a result, she returned home that day and completely cleared her wardrobes and drawers of her overwhelming range of clothes – from a size 8 to 16, as she never knew what size she'd be. What she hadn't realised was that keeping all these clothes undermined her. Once she decided she didn't need to keep them, that she no longer needed to wear baggy tops to cover up, she discarded most and organised what she kept neatly. Getting dressed each morning now makes her smile.

Update your values

Mahatma Gandhi said, 'Your values become your destiny.'[35] That is, our behaviours are driven by our values. We all have values that drive our behaviours around health, personal growth, relationships, career, family and friends, finances. The trouble is, like beliefs, they're often invisible as they tend to have been formed in childhood and have been with us so long, we don't pay them any attention.

They're also influenced by the world around us and personal experience. For example, you may feel you have to follow food trends promoted in the media: clean eating, low-fat foods, juicing, cooking with air fryers. Whether you consider eating as fuel or social time and even what foods you consider enjoyable can be influenced by your childhood experiences. Whether you decide to eat everything on your plate in a restaurant because you've paid for it will be influenced by the values you attribute to money as well as to food.

Have you ever sat down and written out a clear list of your values? Your parents' values from when you were a child may not serve you well as an adult. Yet if you've never consciously considered them, you won't be aware they are driving your eating choices. For example, if you were brought up believing that you should not waste food, you may unconsciously eat everything on your plate, even if you are no longer hungry.

This is a chance to assess and reshape your dietary choices in accordance with the principles that truly resonate with you now. Knowing your values gives you more control over your actions and emotions, allows you to make decisions that serve you better, gives you clarity on what you really need to do to feel good and helps you find alternative ways to fulfil your needs. Making your values conscious and reviewing them will allow you to be successful in your new eating habits. It means you'll make choices that are congruent with what's important to you now and will be more likely to keep the promises you make to yourself. That in turn strengthens your self-belief, and you begin to trust yourself to make the right choices for you.

My story

A family value that served me well as a child was 'eat what you are given'; it was considered respectful to the cook. However, this value adversely affected me as an adult as the trend was for much bigger plates (and, in my case, bowls). In addition, I was eating processed rather than fresh foods, and desserts with higher levels of sugar and fats.

Preventing food waste and respect for the cook are still both important to me, but I show this in different ways. I stop eating as soon as I'm full and put the rest of the food in the fridge for later, or I politely say 'no, thank you' when offered more. Crucially, I have reduced the plate and bowl size at home, which means less gets put in front of me in the first place.

SELF-COACHING ACTIVITY 8:
Identify your values

Consider these conflicting values when you decide to eat:

- Home cooking or convenience
- Your health or eating what you want
- Rewarding yourself with food or feeling energised
- Satisfying your sweet tooth or being slim
- Sitting watching TV or having a healthy heart
- Getting a quick energy fix or having a healthy brain
- Living a short and fun life or living a long and healthy life
- Looking good or feeling good
- Fitting in or being true to you
- Working long hours to achieve business success or looking after your vitality
- Productivity or rest and recuperation
- Eating food for pleasure or eating food to look after your body
- Extreme emotional highs and lows or daily contentment and happiness
- Education to allow choice or blissful ignorance
- Personal growth and challenge or taking the easy route

This list is by no means exhaustive. You may have other conflicting values.

Notice which value you choose versus which one is really more important to you. If your actions and your values are not the same, you are out of alignment. Decide what you will do to change this. If your present eating habits fit your values, stop trying to diet to fit in with the values of others. If your present eating habits aren't in alignment with your true values, then you know it's time to review them and decide which really is more important to you.

Unlock self-empowerment

What if you accepted full responsibility for everything in your life? If you want to have maximum influence in your world, the more responsibility you take, the more control and flexibility you will have, which builds self-respect, self-worth and confidence. This place of personal empowerment in NLP is called being at cause.

The opposite is being at effect. When we are at effect, we see ourselves as victims of our world. Things are happening to us. We blame everything and everyone else; we come up with reasons and excuses, so are powerless to create change. Unless we shift our perception.

When you take responsibility for all the things you can control and work on changing them, letting go of all the things outside of your control, you will feel empowered. I call it escaping the blame frame. It allows you to go from:

- Hopeless ⊠ hopeful

- Self-judgement ⊠ self-acceptance

- Focusing on the problem ⊠ focusing on your solution

- Feeling stuck ⊠ seeing your choices

- Feeling vague about your future ⊠ having clarity

- Procrastinating ⊠ taking action

- Knee-jerk responses ⊠ considered decisions when challenges come your way

- Victim state ⊠ the architect of your life

We can all move in and out of these states at different times and in different situations. Once you become aware of where on this continuum you are at any moment in time, you can then choose what you want to do.

If you are battling with your mind and body to lose weight, simply taking responsibility for the choices you make rather than blaming all the circumstances that have got you where you are now will help you decide on different choices and get different results. You can make a conscious choice on where your energy goes: eating foods and then feeling guilty saps your energy; obsessing about every calorie is draining; flitting from one diet plan to another is exhausting. Continually doing the same thing and not succeeding undermines your self-belief.

If you are harbouring toxic energy – anger, resentment, putting everyone else first, feeling you can't be bothered, delaying what's important – it spills out to your whole life. My experience with clients is that it affects their career and their business as well as their personal relationships. Taking responsibility for who you want to be, and then acting in accordance with that future self may not be the easy route, but it will make you stronger and help you change your relationship with food.

You can also take responsibility for your emotions by acknowledging them and respecting them, rather than ignoring or feeding them. First, consider them on a continuum of low energy to high energy rather than as negative or positive, good or bad. This allows you to accept that emotions just are, and to acknowledge them and pause and decide what you want to do with them. If you can move from low-energy emotions, such as blame and doubt, to higher-energy emotions, like optimism, belief and passion, it improves your wellbeing. You can use this approach to help you lose weight if you acknowledge your emotion and either let it go, act constructively to lessen it or change your belief that feeds it.

When you are stuck in a behaviour no matter what you try, consider if you're affected by secondary gain. All our behaviours have a higher positive intention – that is, we believe on some level that our behaviour is protecting us, keeping us safe. If that resonates, consider how you're benefiting from staying as you are. I look at this in more detail in Chapter 5.

CASE STUDY: TT becomes the architect of her life

TT had been through significant challenges and traumas in her life, both physical and emotional, when she started working with me. Looking at where she was at cause and where she was at effect allowed her to reframe her thoughts about the past and present and to shift out of victim mode. It allowed her to recognise her resilience and build more of it. Importantly, it helped her realise she no longer needed food as a crutch; that she could lose weight and she could find alternative soothers. She then moved into a state of empowerment.

 SELF-COACHING ACTIVITY 9:
Cause and effect

Draw two columns – one for at cause and the other for at effect. List three areas in your life under each and identify how they affect your relationship with food.

 SELF-COACHING ACTIVITY 10:
Alternatives to eating

Once you start to unravel the reasons for holding on to your present eating patterns, when you identify what your unsatisfied emotional need is, you can soothe that need in alternative ways. This is also useful if you use eating as a reward.

Brainstorm a list of activities other than eating that could meet your needs and interests. Some of us forget to play because we are so busy getting everything done, so this could be a great opportunity to put fun on your schedule to restore your energy and create balance. Your activities could include:

- Read a book curled up in a hammock/blanket
- Go for a walk with friends
- Listen to music, sing or dance
- Potter in the garden
- Have a long bath
- Go for a motorbike ride
- Play with the dog
- Do a jigsaw puzzle
- Learn to knit/play an instrument
- Book a massage
- Get your nails done

From your list, choose one that you will do this week instead of eating food.

Grow your self-compassion

How do you respond when you don't do what you intended or promised yourself? Compassion is the ability to understand the emotional state of another person or oneself. It involves taking on a different perspective, putting yourself in someone else's shoes, or disassociating from yourself, looking at yourself from the outside. This allows you to acknowledge that you or they have reasons behind the choices you've made.

Research by Dr Kristin Neff of the University of Texas and her colleagues has shown that self-compassion helps us avoid destructive patterns.[36] When you soothe your emotion with self-compassion, you're better able to notice what's right as well as what's wrong, which allows you to focus on what really brings you joy and make the changes you desire.

Often when we find ourselves eating something we had promised ourselves we wouldn't, or eating too much, or not doing any exercise, or breaking the rules of our diet, we shame ourselves, admonish ourselves, and then we give up completely. You may have spent your life judging yourself, comparing yourself to others and always coming up short. This constant self-criticism, while you may think you're being realistic, is making a situation worse, as you end up feeling inadequate, insecure and incompetent.

Self-compassion is about no longer judging yourself, no longer labelling yourself as 'good' or 'bad', simply accepting yourself as you are and treating yourself with kindness. It is about losing the shame and self-loathing, not allowing yourself the narrative of 'letting yourself down' when you have eaten in a way that you hadn't planned or judging yourself according to the rules others have said are right.

Self-compassion is not an excuse to blindly continue down the path of overeating or self-indulgence, but an opportunity to reflect and consider the positive intention behind the unwanted behaviour. It allows you to be kind to yourself and decide on the best choice open to you now. Only when you're kind to yourself rather than blaming, berating or beating yourself up will you make the best choices for you in moments of difficulty.

According to Neff, one way to notice your levels of self-compassion is to think about how you respond to others who are struggling in a way similar to you, perhaps a friend. Notice what you typically do, say, feel and think when you're responding to them, and then think about how you typically respond to yourself in the same situation. Perhaps you'll notice a difference, and if you do, ask yourself how things may change if you responded to yourself in the same way you respond to your friend.

Self-compassion and self-acceptance are essential to create peace and balance with food, because we make more helpful and kinder choices when we feel loved and accepted. One way to build self-love is to put yourself first. We often grow up with the belief that putting ourselves first is selfish, yet to have the health and body you want requires you meet your needs first, not being swayed from your path by other people's eating needs or desires, their social plans, their routines, their deadlines. By meeting your own needs first, you can let go of your old food habits and start to eat what your body needs, when it wants it, and in a way that you truly enjoy. This is about creating healthy boundaries, protecting yourself and your needs, so that you can help others more effectively, as you are fully nourished and coming from a place of personal strength.

SELF-COACHING ACTIVITY 11: Boundaries

Draw up a list of the people whose needs you address each day. Rank them in the order you prioritise them, and then ask yourself these questions:

- What would happen if you put yourself at the top of your list?
- What would you have to change to do so?
- What boundaries would you need to put in place?

My story

For me, adopting self-compassion was significant when I was tired and busy. I'd often find myself craving something sweet, so I'd use self-compassion to decide what was really the best choice for me in that moment. For example, I may have decided that a chunk of chocolate would be an acceptable immediate fix and an early night was the solution for later.

> *I used an NLP principle as a mantra to interrupt negative thoughts about myself: 'Everyone is doing the best they can with the resources available to them at the time'. This allowed me to accept my choice was the best available to me at the time and move on rather than stress or be critical about it.*

 SELF-COACHING ACTIVITY 12:
Self-compassion scale

Determine where you are on the self-compassion scale. Notice how you typically act towards yourself in challenging times, and with that awareness you can boost your self-compassion and start changing your relationship with food and dieting.

For each statement, rate how often you adopt the behaviour using the scale 1–5, where 1 is almost never and 5 is almost always:

1. When I fail at something, I become overwhelmed by thoughts and feelings of not being good enough.

2. I try to accept those aspects of my personality I don't like.

3. When something challenging happens, I try to reframe the situation.

4. When I'm feeling low, I think everyone else is happier than me.

5. I try to see failure as part of life and the learning process.

6. When life is tough, I am kind and gentle with myself.

7. When something or someone upsets me, I try to keep my emotions in balance.

8. When I fail at something, I think I'm the only one in the situation.

9. When I'm feeling low, I tend to focus on everything that's not working.

10. When I feel not good enough in some way, I try to remind myself that everyone feels that way at some point.

11. I am critical and judgemental about myself.

12. I'm intolerant of and irritated by aspects of my personality I don't like.

Now, calculate your self-compassion score:

- Reverse score questions 1,4,8,9,11,12, so 1=5, 2=4, 3=3, 4=2, 5=1.

- Add up your total score and divide it by twelve, which gives you your self-compassion score. Between 2.5 and 3.5 is a moderate score.

This exercise was adapted from Kristin Neff's short-form self-compassion scale quiz.[37]

Now you know your score, consider how you could start to grow your self-compassion. Use the 'Affirmation' Self-coaching Activity in the next chapter to develop a mantra you could say to yourself in those moments where your self-compassion is lowest and most likely to trigger you into sabotaging your new eating habits.

Summary

In this chapter, we have started our inner declutter. We have explored how we can change the beliefs and values that are influencing our eating patterns in unhelpful ways and sabotaging our attempts to eat more healthily. We have also explored how self-compassion is key to our self-improvement.

In the next chapter, we will look at changing our thinking as it is our thoughts that trigger our beliefs and, in turn, our feelings, and then that creates our eating patterns. Where changing your beliefs is primarily about having self-compassion, changing your thinking is about being optimistic and constructive.

FOUR
Think Yourself Slim

A re your thought patterns constructive or destructive? Our brain is constantly in motion, thinking. Our thoughts both reflect and create our reality, becoming the stories we tell ourselves. The beliefs we looked at in the last chapter are created from thoughts that are repeated over and over, but just because we think something doesn't mean it is true.

Our thoughts also reflect and affect our speech and actions. It's no surprise, therefore, they are key to our success, yet we often let them go unnoticed. When we learn to notice our thoughts, we can become more aware of their impact on how we feel, how we behave, the choices we make – and we can change them.

Use this chapter to be curious about your thinking habits and clear out what is unhelpful and undermines you to create more positive thinking. Positive thinking is not about ignoring mistakes or your perceived reality, but about reframing what has happened or is happening to be more optimistic and constructive.

Retrain your inner voice

How aware are you of your inner dialogue? According to research, we have 6,200 thoughts in a day,[38] yet one negative thought can create a spiral of negative thinking for the rest of the day, a week or even longer. At best, this is demotivating, and at its worst, it leads to us sabotaging ourselves – perhaps by eating more with the excuse of 'What's the point?' Negative thinking can undermine our attempts to lose weight and even prevent us from starting our diet.

The quality of your thoughts and ultimately your identity is impacted by your language. If you choose words with a negative bias, then you will perpetuate negative thinking. Negative thinking is exhausting and demotivating. Repetitive negative thinking lowers your mood and reduces your self-belief.[39] In contrast, healthy thinking patterns improve your quality of life. Positive thinking not only lifts your mood in the moment, it helps you make more empowered decisions.

Our thoughts are not reality, but they create our reality. If you have spent a lifetime using words such as lazy/stupid/rubbish to describe yourself, this is what will show up in your world. If you choose to change your vocabulary to less judgemental and more optimistic language, then this will be reflected in the quality of your thinking, how you feel and your behaviour choices.

Why not choose language that creates the reality you want? Thoughts that are hopeful, that open you to a life of possibility and abundance? The unconscious mind cannot tell the difference between reality and something that you have imagined, so you can feed your brain what you want it to believe.

We all have an inner voice, and it may work for us or against us. You've been practising your thoughts for years so they may be invisible to you, even though they are what sabotages you. You may have become more aware of your inner voice over time, or you may be so aware of her you have even given her a name.

There is nothing wrong with inner chatter. It's only an issue when you aren't aware of its influence and if it is an inner critic rather than an inner guru. For example, when you get something wrong, an inner critic will put you down, name-call or play the blame game, whereas an inner guru will validate you, calm you and encourage resilience.

When we are critical or judgemental about ourselves, we tend to resist change, because we see it as us needing to be fixed. This doesn't motivate us; it hinders us. Whereas, when we speak kindly to ourselves and have self-compassion, we are more likely to embrace self-improvement. This positive self-regard is key to changing our relationship with food.

Our fears around judgement of our body weight can create a negative loop in our head that affects our confidence: we think we don't look good, so we worry that others think we don't look good, and then we rehearse the snap judgements people may make about us. Especially given the stereotyping and body shaming that goes on in the media.

If we have that negative loop, if we are afraid of being imperfect, the resultant lack of confidence may impact on our relationships, our social life or our income. We're less likely to put ourselves forward for something if we don't look how we believe we should, and we don't show up with the right mindset when we do put ourselves forward as we are already preparing ourselves for failure and rejection, and we project this image out into the world. Our personal identity starts to fade, be it at work or in our own business, at home or where we hang out.

Once you become aware of your inner voice, you can start to change it or challenge it, which allows you to be more flexible and adaptable. Although it may be tempting to argue with your inner voice, for me, that lacks compassion. I would advocate soothing the voice. If unhelpful thoughts pop into your mind, you can thank your voice for her old wisdom and let her know you have moved on, and then gently brush the voice away. Remember, like beliefs, thoughts are not facts, and you can choose different ones.

You can make your inner critic into your cheerleader. When you change how she sounds and what she says, you can begin to create an inner guru who will help you feel secure within yourself.

Challenging your thoughts is just like challenging your beliefs. You need to:

- Provide evidence to the contrary when an unhelpful or critical thought pops into your head

- Respond with positive thoughts about you and what you love about you

- Create a positive affirmation that focuses on what you want instead

When you change your thinking, you will start to influence your body.

CASE STUDY: Karen's act of kindness

A client, Karen, was very aware her inner voice sabotaged her eating goals. After setting an ambitious goal, despite not really being interested in cooking and food, she would quickly find herself off track and immediately speak unkindly to herself. She would then go into 'I don't care' mode and not follow her plan.

Karen wanted to get off this rollercoaster. She decided to make it more about the journey than the destination and created kinder responses to use as mantras in difficult moments and affirmations to develop more self-love and self-care. It felt uncomfortable, but she knew it was key to being able to achieve the body she wanted, as valuing herself and what she put in her body was essential to being happy.

SELF-COACHING ACTIVITY 13:
Change your Inner Voice

Close your eyes and notice what your inner voice sounds like, where it is located and what sort of things it says.

If you have a quietly confident voice, one who is shyly saying things to encourage you, perhaps she's your younger self. How about turning her up in volume? Could you move her further forward and more central? Make her stronger, louder, more assertive? This is the woman who will propel you forward, help you achieve your dreams.

If you have a doubting or nagging voice, one who is questioning every decision you make, telling you that you can't do this, could you make the voice quieter or softer? Could you change the sound of the voice to one with more positive connotations, one that lifts you or makes you laugh? Could you turn the volume down? Could you move her off to the side of your head or to somewhere less intrusive?

Perhaps you could name her if you haven't already. Perhaps you could befriend her, accept her and respond to her in the way you would a friend who gave you unhelpful advice.

Rewire your thinking

What if you only had supportive and constructive thoughts? By practising new ways of thinking, you can change the way your brain works, upgrade your thoughts and build new eating habits.

The unconscious mind needs repetition to create new neural pathways and install a new habit. The more you practise positive thinking, the quicker you will reprogramme your unconscious mind. Two excellent techniques for this are saying affirmations and practising gratitude.

An affirmation is a phrase that is spoken out loud repeatedly to motivate you and change your thinking about you. Phrased in the first person (I) and the present tense, as if you already are that person, an affirmation shifts your identity. When said regularly and repeatedly, the message becomes ingrained in your unconscious and your mind believes it to be true.

Affirmations are positive, kind and goal oriented. Avoid phrases like 'losing weight' as loss is a negative. Never use the word 'not' as it means you're focusing on what you don't want; instead, be clear on what you do want. Don't talk about how you want to look; rather, focus on how you want to feel.

Your affirmation is designed to create a thought and belief you want to have. If your present belief is a long way from what you want to believe, create an affirmation that takes you some way towards the desired belief, which you can then make stronger later. Using an affirmation that is too far from your present state causes you to doubt yourself, and that will only result in more negativity. Saying thank you at the beginning of your affirmations is a great way of acting 'as if', as you are telling yourself that you are already enjoying something.

Practise only one or two affirmations at a time as this will help your unconscious mind to focus on what you want and set you up for success. Once you have accepted your affirmation to be true, you can create yourself a new one to move your thinking to the next level. When you focus on where you want to go rather than where you have been, you create a new thinking pattern that increases your optimism and helps change your belief system more quickly.

Consider when you will say your affirmations. I love saying mine first thing in the morning to set my day up for success and last thing at night to create positive thoughts as I drift off to sleep. In addition, you can use them any time you feel drawn to behave in old ways that could sabotage your new thinking habits.

Practising gratitude is a powerful tool for creating the state of happiness. Gratitude changes how you think about yourself and your world around you – for the better. Research has shown that it can help improve your relationship with food and exercise.[40]

When life is making you feel challenged or when you need encouragement to keep going with your new eating plan, focusing on what you are thankful for is an excellent activity. Some people like to do this to focus their mind in the morning, others like to do this at night as it helps them drop off to sleep quickly and easily, and sleep is crucial to your wellbeing.

You can write down or speak out loud what you are grateful for, whichever works better for you, although writing often has a stronger impact. This is a long-term strategy that is very straightforward and has an amazing impact on your self-perception and your optimism. A gratitude journal is a great ritual to celebrate your progress in changing your relationship with yourself and with food as it is tracking your thinking and feeling over time.

It's the small habits that create change, so your gratitude journal celebrates what you have achieved to foster your self-belief and build your confidence. As the saying goes, be grateful for where you're at and excited by where you're going.

 SELF-COACHING ACTIVITY 14:
Affirmations

To create new thinking patterns and lift your mood in low moments, follow these steps to create an empowering affirmation:

1. Write down as many affirmations as you can think of that could support the change you want to make.
2. Say them out loud and really listen to the words as you speak them, noticing which feel better than others.
3. Change or add words to make each affirmation perfect for you.
4. Choose the one that feels best, the one that lifts you to the next level of thinking and aspiration.
5. Write your affirmation on Post-it notes and stick them to your bathroom mirror, your fridge, your wardrobe door – absolutely anywhere you can think of that will trigger the thoughts you want. You can even have it as your screensaver.

Here are some affirmation suggestions to get you started:

- Today, I easily choose to nourish my mind and body.
- My mind and body are becoming healthier and fitter every day.
- Today, I am full of energy and joy.

- My eating choices are becoming easier and smarter every day.
- My thoughts are filled with positivity and my life is full of promise.
- Everything I do now will create the future I want.
- I am growing stronger every day.
- I love myself unconditionally and I am always kind to myself.
- Today, I fully enjoy the life-giving energy of nutritious foods.
- More and more, I listen to how my body feels and what it truly needs.
- I know I have all the resources I need to...

 SELF-COACHING ACTIVITY 15:
Gratitude

However you choose to practise gratitude is the perfect way for you. You may buy a special gratitude notebook, write everything you're grateful for in your planner or your journal, record your gratitudes on your phone or write them on pieces of paper and keep them in a jar, or simply say them out loud.

Aim to record between three and ten gratitudes each day. Include things you are great at, what you've enjoyed doing that day, any small achievement. If you get stuck, list the simpler things: sunrise, a blue sky, birdsong, rain, the air you breathe, the bed you sleep in, a hot shower, the food on your table, your nourishment, the unconditional love of your pet, child or parent. Nature is always abundant, so it is a great place to look for the positives in your world.

Each morning, reread the previous day's gratitudes to start your day positively.

Adjust how you talk about food

How many phrases can you think of linked to dieting? Language gives us the key to our world: it shapes and reflects our thinking. Your language may impart confidence about your life and yourself, or it may place limitations on your life.

As part of your inner declutter, I will guide you to consider how the language around food and weight loss impacts you. I'll show you how this language can be judgemental and, therefore, how you may have come to struggle with your relationship with food and yourself.

When I listen to women talking about why they want to lose weight, they frequently say, 'I just don't want to be fat'. As a society, we have become very fattist, and having any amount of body fat seems to be a crime and is associated with shame. At the same time, we are bombarded with manufactured foods that have little nutritional value, yet which increase body fat.

Personally, I don't use the adjective 'fat' and loathe 'obese'. Even 'overweight' is bothersome, as who determines what is normal to judge what's over-weight? There are many reasons why normal may be different for each of us: gender, genetics, bone structure, metabolism, ethnicity and age for starters. However, when we don't fit someone else's normal, it can make us feel not good enough, lesser. This is dangerous.

Men have controlled the fashion industry and art for years, so what is considered the right weight or shape for women is seen through their eyes, the male gaze. Models have starved themselves and used drugs like cocaine to stave off hunger so that they can meet the popular body shape of the time. We see that influ-ence through Kate Moss, who is infamous for saying, 'Nothing tastes as good as skinny feels.'[41] Today, we contend with airbrushing and filters used on images that promote a particular look and can make us feel inadequate.

As women, we have been taught to compare our-selves to other women according to looks, and that includes our size. We congratulate women on losing weight, commenting on their appearance and judging them according to some standard set by the patriar-chy. Instead of focusing on size and weight, we should focus instead on having more energy, more confidence and improved wellbeing.

When we hear the word 'diet', most of us think of deprivation, starvation, feeling left out, looking for low-fat labels, weighing and calorie counting. Even the phrase 'I'm on a diet' is how we respond when we believe we can't eat or don't want to eat the food that is on offer because it's 'not on the plan' or 'it's fattening'.

A key technique for changing your diet mindset is to change how you think about the word 'diet'. Diet actually encompasses what we have in our life, the nutrition and nourishment we give our whole self. It's the choices we make on a daily basis, not a state of deprivation or following a regime to lose weight for a few days, weeks or months. 'Losing weight' is a problematic phrase, because why would we want to lose something? Our unconscious mind certainly wouldn't.

The whole paradigm of going on a diet and losing weight is a false focus for the purpose of eating and represents in and of itself a relationship with food that has gone awry. Food should be our friend as it is what gives us life and energy. Instead, it has become our enemy, about control.

Perhaps you talk about falling off the wagon when you don't get your eating 'right'. This idiom bothers me because it comes from a place of negativity – the idea of failing, and failing at someone else's rules. Not exactly life affirming. Another one is being 'off track', which is associated with making a mistake, such as when you have chosen to celebrate special occasions and they've all come at once. Reframed, this is about balance: you have been honouring your values by attending important events and your 'occasional' foods on your pyramid (see Self-coaching Activity 16) have tipped to the 'sometimes' category because there have been so many. All that needs to happen is you return to your normal.

Do you think you're treating or spoiling yourself when you have a biscuit or a glass of wine? A treat is something out of the ordinary that gives you great pleasure, for example, quality time with loved ones, inspiration, adventure, whereas to spoil is to diminish the value of or harm, for example when you're over-eating or overindulging. Indulging in itself is about forsaking control and responsibility.

Our choice of word or phrase affects our outcome. Other guilt-laden vocabulary associated with eating that you could choose to change to shift your thinking and improve your relationship with food includes:

- **Cheating:** You are not cheating; you are choosing an alternative, allowing balance in your life.

- **Being naughty:** You are not being naughty; you're eating a food that it is fine to eat occasionally.

Dieting culture is synonymous with 'good' and 'bad', two words that trigger unhelpful thinking patterns. There is nothing that's inherently either good or bad – it's just our thinking that makes it so. You don't have good and bad days; you just have days. Some days you are focused and energised, some days you are tired, overwhelmed or hormonal.

If you view foods in terms of good and bad, you probably think you should eat good foods and not bad foods. You may feel bad if you eat bad foods and only feel good if you eat good foods. Categorising food in terms of good or bad is not helpful as it sets up a dichotomy that creates a simplistic and hostile relationship with food.

If we apply this good/bad principle to three foods, avocados, walnuts and juice, we can see how it's not helpful. Avocado is beneficial to your health with its monounsaturated fat, potassium, vitamins, fibre and antioxidants, but many diets avoid avocados because they are high in calories (approximately the same as a small bar of chocolate). However, they are full of goodness and keep us full for far longer than the chocolate. This could help with weight loss.

The National Health and Examination Survey 2001–2008 found that people who consume avocados have a significantly lower body mass index, waist circumference and body weight.[42] Avocado consumption is associated with improved overall diet quality, nutrient intake and a reduced risk of metabolic syndrome, stroke and type 2 diabetes.

Nuts are high in calories yet have many nutritional benefits. Walnuts, for example, provide healthy fats, fibre, vitamins, omega 3 and minerals. In fact, they're so amazing there is a conference in California each year to discuss the latest walnut health research. It is believed they assist with appetite control and weight loss, and that they affect our brain in a way that helps us resist more highly tempting food.[43]

Fruit juice is considered by many to be one of their five (portions of fruit and vegetables) a day because of the vitamins, and some people follow a juicing or cleansing diet. Nutritionists argue juicing loses the benefits of the fruit's fibre while elevating your blood sugars more quickly, so fruit juice should be drunk sparingly.[44]

From this, we can see that choosing what to eat is not as straightforward as good and bad, so what are alternative words to use? If your goal is a balanced diet that maintains wellbeing and a healthy weight and body shape, it's more helpful to categorise foods in terms of when you can eat them – never, rarely, occasionally, sometimes, often or always – or in terms of portion size – those where it is beneficial to eat a small, medium or generous portion. Alternatively, you could think of foods in terms of what they give you – energising, nutritious, luxurious, celebratory – or in terms of type of food – manufactured or homemade, preserved or fresh, energy dense or nutrient dense, organic or farmed. These categories provide you with more information and more choice.

SELF-COACHING ACTIVITY 16:
Food pyramid

The following exercise is based on an idea shared with me by my nutritionist colleague Jennifer Williams.

Create a pyramid with six layers. Label the bottom layer 'Always'. Label the next layer 'Often', with 'Sometimes', 'Occasionally', 'Rarely' as you go up. At the top is 'Never'. Write in specific foods you want to eat in each frequency to create balance.

You could also create other graphics. For example, draw a circle to represent a plate and divide it into three sections to represent small, medium and generous portions. Write the foods you decide are appropriate in each section.

CASE STUDY: TT's shift with the pyramid

TT was struggling to let go of foods that she wanted to eat as she enjoyed them. Also, from years of dieting, she had lost sight of what would help her lose weight and what wouldn't.

She found it really liberating to create a food pyramid where she was choosing her foods in a truly different way to dieting rules. She felt more empowered and could decide what to eat more easily. The pyramid helped her aim for the balance she desired in her life, as she could choose to add foods to her 'Always' level and, rather than removing food from her diet, move it higher up the levels. She felt happier knowing she had choice and she could stop feeling like she was cheating. TT decided that for her there were no 'Never' foods; it was all about balance.

Get specific with your thinking

Do you know which words trigger you? Changing your language is transformational. Once you observe how your language drives your emotions and your decisions, you are empowered to change both it and your outcomes.

The adjectives 'good' and 'bad' are likely to be generalised to other areas of your life, not just food. As they are judgemental rather than reflective, they will potentially sabotage you. Typical phrases you may use at the end of another day of feeling disillusioned with trying to diet are 'I've had a bad day' or 'I've been bad today'. Often, this means you have generalised one experience or one choice to a whole day or your whole person. The word 'bad' creates a low energy, which is unhelpful. It is also non-specific, so erodes your ability to evaluate the situation and avoid repeating it.

For example, if you say, 'I had a bad day, my boss made me eat a piece of cake', you are blaming your boss for your behaviour and generalising your disappointment in yourself for that one choice to your whole day. If you use more specific language, you can uncover the choices you made and take responsibility for what is yours to change should a similar situation occur again. For example, 'My boss chose to speak rudely, so I chose to eat a piece of cake to soothe my hurt. I was then annoyed at myself for that choice all day.'

When we accept that other people's behaviour is all about them, we can respond differently in the moment, perhaps no longer needing to soothe our hurt feelings with food. If we do choose to eat, we can practise self-compassion.

'I've been bad today' translates as 'I'm a bad person', which is about your identity. When you link your behaviour to your identity, it has a very strong influence on your self-perception. The two little words 'I am' are so powerful as they create our identity and can lead to a negative spiral when used in an unhelpful way.

For example, 'I've been so bad today. I forgot my lunch and grabbed a meal deal with cake. Now I feel really fat. I'm so rubbish.' If you ask yourself, 'How specifically have I been bad?' and break the situation down, it will give you more helpful feedback that allows for compassion and change. 'I was late and forgot my lunch today, so I bought a cheap meal deal, but it included crisps and cake. That means I've eaten too many unhealthy fats, salts, sugars and additives today. However, I was late because I was finishing a project, which has reduced my stress. I noticed I didn't feel as full as usual after lunch and started to feel sluggish later, so I will make sure I pack my lunch tonight.'

Escape your thinking traps

Do you undermine your plans by negotiating with yourself? You know the kind of thing:

- Just this one won't hurt.

- If I treat myself now, I'll eat a smaller dinner tonight.

- I went for a walk this morning, so I can have pizza for dinner.

- I'll do my sit-ups after work as I'm late this morning.

My main traps were, 'I'll make my lunch in the morning so that I can go to bed now because I'm too tired,' and then the next day, 'I'll just have another five minutes in bed and buy a lunch.'

When we negotiate with ourselves, when we allow ourselves to change our plan, we are planning to fail. We sabotage our good intentions. When we are clear on our purpose, it is easier to keep our commitment to ourselves. If you value yourself and your plan, you will be able to shift your old habit of negotiating with yourself.

Notice what your self-negotiation habits are. If you have a bias towards a particular thought or a common trigger, come up with an answer to your thought or create a stock phrase to bat the thought away with – one that encourages you and gets you focused on achieving your goal. For example, 'Do it now, you'll thank yourself later'.

Gretchen Rubin, creator of the Happiness Project, calls these thinking traps 'Loopholes' and has put them into ten categories,[45] which I will share in the table below as I find them to be a helpful framework for challenging our thinking. From an NLP perspective, it is a meta model that reveals how we have filtered our experience through our language and helps us look more closely to allow us to recover the choices we have made around food.

This model shines a light on the rules and limits you have imposed on your thinking. When you start analysing your thinking in this way, it's like you're being woken from a trance and given a pair of glasses through which you can see yourself and the world more clearly. I've given examples of how I've used the loopholes, as well as other examples to look out for, and for each loophole, a strategy to challenge your mindset.

LOOPHOLE FRAMEWORK

Loophole: False choice

Explanation: Suggests it has to be either/or when it doesn't. Characterised by 'If... then...' and 'because'.

My example: I can either enjoy life to the fullest, or eat lettuce and carrots for the rest of my life.

Other examples

- If I eat healthily, then I don't enjoy the meal.
- I don't have time to cook because I'm too busy with work.
- If I stay by the food at a party, then I won't have to talk to anyone.
- I can't do that because I need to lose weight first.
- If I could drop a dress size, then I'd have more confidence.
- I can't eat healthily because I need energy to focus.

Strategy to challenge your thinking: Is it true? What other choices can you make? Is there a compromise?

Check in with your true values if you are using this thinking and look at what you are avoiding.

Loophole: Moral licensing

Explanation: Giving ourselves permission to do something 'bad' because we've been 'good'.

My example: I've worked hard all week, so I've earned myself a slap-up meal and a few drinks tonight.

Other examples

- I've been so good today, I can have a bigger portion.
- I've followed the diet all week, so I can have the weekend off and eat what I want.
- I was good and didn't have a starter, so I can have dessert like everyone else.
- I was up late working, so I need coffee and cake to get me through the day.

Strategy to challenge your thinking: Update your language and reframe what you're saying, and be clear and honest with what you're deciding. The Pareto (80/20) Principle, discussed in Chapter 7, may be helpful to guide your thinking here, as well as finding alternative rewards.

Loophole: Tomorrow

Explanation: When we plan for our future selves, we have good intentions. Yet we don't look out for our present selves.

My example: I'll start my diet in the school holidays when I have more energy.

Other examples

- Tomorrow, I'll be good. I'll draw a line under today and start again.
- I promise I'll go to the gym next week as I need to work late today.
- When I've used up all the goodies in the cupboard, it'll be easier.
- I'll go to the fitness club next week. Today, I want to enjoy a special dinner and watch a film.

Strategy to challenge your thinking: Ask yourself what you really want for you *now* as every day counts. Then decide what you want to do – take action. Be kind to yourself and be balanced every day.

Loophole: Lack of control

Explanation: When we're deluding ourselves, we don't have control over our actions.

My example: If there is cake when I get my coffee, I can't resist eating it.

Other examples

- I'm too stressed to keep to a diet.
- I can't help myself when I drink wine.
- I eat when I'm bored.
- It's impossible to give up sugar when I need energy.
- I wish they wouldn't supply biscuits at these long meetings.

Strategy to challenge your thinking: Pause and remind yourself that you *do* have choices. Ask yourself which is the right choice for you. Focus on how you will feel an hour after your choice.

Loophole: Planning to fail

Explanation: When we make a decision that on the surface is unrelated to ourselves and/or our plan, or so we tell ourselves, but results in us being in the exact situation we wanted to avoid.

My example: I'll just do this last task on my to-do list before I go to my Pilates class... Now I'm too late because I've missed the warm-up.

Other examples

- I'll buy biscuits in case someone else wants them.
- I'll just pop to Marks & Spencer to buy a new dress as I've lost weight... and I end up buying their cheesecake.
- We love to go all-inclusive on holiday so we can truly relax, and I can't resist the all-you-can-eat food.

Strategy to challenge your thinking: Call yourself out on your behaviour when you're sabotaging yourself. Accept and acknowledge it with compassion, and then plan to interrupt the behaviour before you start it next time.

Loophole: 'This doesn't count'

Explanation: Some of us create special rules to excuse our behaviours – going off grid, get-out-of-jail cards, what happens in Vegas stays in Vegas.

My example: It's the school holidays. Time to relax and de-stress.

Other examples

- There's only a small bit left and it's a shame to throw it away.
- They made it specially for me.
- It's a diet version.
- I don't even want it.
- When in Rome...

Strategy to challenge your thinking: When creating your goal, decide what you are going to do – what is acceptable to you – ahead of time. Be realistic, be balanced, be honest and stick to it.

Loophole: Questionable assumption

Explanation: Consciously or unconsciously, we make assumptions that influence our habits – and when we have made them a while ago, they become invisible.

My example: I need to eat it all to get good value when I eat out.

Other examples

- The label looks healthy.
- I have to finish my to-do list before I grab lunch.
- I've got so much weight to lose, there's no point in trying.
- If I eat this, my craving will be satisfied, and I'll stop.
- All my friends struggle with their weight.
- Chocolate makes me feel good.

Strategy to challenge your thinking: Ask yourself, 'When did I decide that?' Be honest with yourself in the moment and make a decision that serves you well. Invest time to create a new behaviour.

Loophole: Concern for others

Explanation: We often tell ourselves that we're acting out of consideration for others. Maybe we are – and maybe we aren't.

My example: It would be rude not to eat the dinner he has made me.

Other examples

- At my networking meeting, it would seem unsociable if I didn't eat and drink too.

- If they've taken the time to cook it, then I should eat it.
- I can't leave my grandson to eat a McDonald's on his own.
- I can't join that exercise group because it's when my family needs me at home.

Strategy to challenge your thinking: Prioritise your wellbeing. Learn to put yourself first and say a positive no. Come up with an alternative strategy. Give others time to adapt to your new habits – people don't like us to change.

Loophole: Fake self-actualisation

Explanation: We delude ourselves we're making the most of life, but actually we're avoiding the challenge of change.

My example: We don't come to this restaurant often, so why shouldn't I...?

Other examples

- I love life too much to deprive myself of this.
- This always makes me feel better.
- It's Friyay!
- It's sunny for once. I've got to have a beer to celebrate.
- It's today's special, so the restaurant might not have it again (fear of missing out – FOMO).
- I have to die of something.

Strategy to challenge your thinking: Build habits that will make you happy long term. Decide what you are willing to give up in the present to create the future you want. Demand more from yourself. Have a clear visualised goal and an accountability system.

Loophole: One coin

Explanation: This is thus named as Rubin relates it to Dutch Theologian Desiderius Erasmus's musings in his 1511 work *Praise of Folly*[46] that if a man believes the ten coins he starts out with won't make him rich and keeps adding one coin to the pile, he has to consider the fact that at some point, there will be one coin that will make him rich.

My example: One cake won't matter.

Other examples

- A year from now what I ate today won't matter.
- I've been bad on my diet this week, so there's no point in going to my slimming group.
- What difference does it make if I spend this afternoon going for a walk or reading?
- In for a penny, in for a pound.

Strategy to challenge your thinking: Focus on micro gains, the concept that small steps add up, as detailed by James Clear in his book *Atomic Habits*.[47] Whether you focus on the coin or the growing heap of coins will shape your behaviour. One coin – or biscuit or cake or beer – is inconsequential, but the habit matters. Observe how often you have the thought that one won't matter and how you act on it. Record your successes so you don't give up. Also, beware others using it to sabotage you. A possible reply is: 'You're right, having one biscuit is no big deal – and I'm not going to have one today.'

 SELF-COACHING ACTIVITY 17:
Thinking loopholes

List the loopholes on a piece of paper or a document on your computer, or download my workbook using the QR code at the end of the book. Highlight each one with red if you use it a lot, amber if you've been known to use it and green if that's not you. Add examples of the phrases you use that could sabotage you.

Create a plan to interrupt those loopholes you have highlighted in red or amber, or decide what you will say to yourself to challenge the phrase you currently use.

Create an abundance mindset

In NLP, we learn to focus on what we want rather than what we don't want, as we get more of what we focus on. Creating an abundance mindset rather than a scarcity mindset[48] supports us to do this as we reprogramme our unconscious mind to think positively.

An abundance mindset is about growth: it comes from a place of optimism and allows you to see more possibilities, options and alternatives. You assume everyone is doing the best they can with the resources they have available. It allows you to be more flexible and therefore more successful. By contrast, a scarcity mindset is about limitations: it comes from a place of fear and focuses on lack. You see everything and everyone in the world as competition, so you compare yourself to others. Our brains have a negative bias, so it is easy to stay stuck in a scarcity mindset.[49]

Cultivating an abundance mindset allows you to feel happy, secure and confident, no matter your circumstance, and the techniques in this chapter help you rewire your brain to do this.[50] A scarcity mindset keeps you in a yo-yo dieting pattern, feeling desperate, swinging to extreme ends of the pendulum as you compare yourself to others and self-sabotage. On the other hand, when you develop abundant thinking, you can have a more healthy relationship with food and yourself. It allows you to move from being at effect to being at cause – an empowered state.

Desperate dieter	Empowered eater
You diet because you 'should'. You limit your food intake because you think you should look a certain way.	You focus on nourishing your body so that you can feel well and live a long and happy life.
You see yourself as a victim, doomed to be overweight, and blame your weight on lack of willpower, a poor metabolism or your genetic make-up.	You see yourself as the architect of your life and take responsibility for the food you eat and your lifestyle. You are clear on your values and make aligned eating choices.

(Continued)

(Cont.)

Desperate dieter	Empowered eater
You weigh yourself constantly when you're dieting. You swing from dieting obsessively to eating out of disappointment/shame/self-loathing. You yo-yo diet constantly.	You rarely weigh yourself. You eat a balanced diet and choose the food your body needs when it needs it. You eat for a purpose.
You're a fussy, picky or obsessive eater. You're reluctant to try new foods because you think you won't like them. Your first question is, 'How many calories are in it?'	You like trying new foods and you're open to new ways of eating – life is an adventure. You enjoy breaking bread with others.
You consider foods to be good and bad. You justify your poor food choices to yourself and force yourself to eat foods you consider good all the while feeling deprived because you can't have what you enjoy.	You believe all food has a place, just in different frequencies or amounts. You aim to feel balance and choose foods you enjoy.
You worry every time you eat in case you put on weight. You feel guilty after you've eaten something not on your plan.	You enjoy each mouthful of food and focus on what it does for your body. You can eat luxury foods once in a while with no self-judgement.
You have a cortisol belly from stress. You're always tired. You feel unfit and avoid exercise. You may be diabetic or pre-diabetic. You hide behind baggy clothes.	You feel well, balanced and energised. You enjoy having some form of movement in your life. You walk and dress proudly and with confidence.

Desperate dieter	Empowered eater
You compare your body weight and shape to others, seeing where you aren't as good as them. You're disappointed if you gain a pound or only lose a pound. Your energy and focus is on losing weight.	You accept your body is unique. You appreciate your health and accept your imperfections. You celebrate each improvement to your wellbeing.
You have little control around food and often eat to please others. You don't stop eating until your food is gone. You struggle to practise delayed gratification and you suffer from FOMO.	You are aware of your triggers. You listen to your body and eat when you're hungry and refuse foods politely when you're not. You stop eating when you feel satisfied, knowing there is more food whenever you need it.
You've been on so many diets you're confused by which foods you should eat. You over-plan your food and then don't stick to it because it doesn't inspire you.	You have clarity on which foods are nutritious. You have an overview of what foods you want to eat over the week and when you will eat them. For the most part, you keep to your plan.
You focus on your faults and your 'mistakes'. You sabotage your efforts when they are not perfect enough.	You practise self-compassion and see failure only as feedback and an opportunity to learn more about yourself.
You think you can't afford to eat healthily and that you don't have time to cook, so you buy cheap refined and processed foods that bulk you up and are quick to prepare.	You choose to eat less, but better-quality foods, and invest money in foods that boost your wellbeing. You make time to seek out easy and quick-to-cook recipes that you will enjoy.

SELF-COACHING ACTIVITY 18:
Empowered eater strategies

Copy out the empowered eater categories and highlight the thoughts and behaviours you already do in green – these are to be celebrated. Copy the desperate dieter categories and highlight the thoughts and behaviours you definitely do in red and those you sometimes do in amber.

Rewrite your scarcity thoughts into abundance statements so that you can interrupt your thought or behaviour when you notice it. Remember to be kind and compassionate.

CASE STUDY: Debra created balance in her eating

Debra focused on two of the traits of a desperate dieter that for her intertwined:

1. You consider food to be good or bad.
2. You sabotage your efforts when they are not perfect enough.

Building on her understanding that she spent life at the two ends of the yo-yo pendulum we discussed in Chapter 2, she recognised that accepting all food is OK would be significant for her. Developing self-compassion and embracing the art of reframing would allow her to respond differently in unexpected eating situations. With these new perspectives, she was able to create balance: she could choose to have more chocolate than usual or have different food on holiday without resorting to all-or-nothing thinking and sabotaging her otherwise healthy eating because she had been 'bad'.

Not failure, feedback

When we're struggling to make a change, it is easy to forget that imperfection is integral to the learning process, it's a feature of the journey of change. When you do get something 'wrong', remember there is no such thing as failure, only feedback. If you let go of the notion of failure and embrace the idea of experimenting instead, you will be able to shift from all-or-nothing thinking and stop sabotaging yourself.

How do you respond to failure? As a learner, you could ask yourself what led to that moment, what you could do differently next time, and reflect on how you could support yourself to make this change more easily. If you develop compassion for yourself in those moments, you acknowledge that this is a struggle, that struggle is a feature of change, that others also struggle. Failure is only when you give up.

One small word that reflects this struggle with food when something doesn't quite go right is 'but'. For example:

- I started off OK, but then it went downhill.

- I'd like to go out for dinner, but I'm on a diet.

- There's so much fat in a cappuccino I shouldn't have one, but I don't care.

- I need to go for a run, but I don't have time.

If you notice 'but' creeping into your thinking, be more specific and change it to 'and', which will help you focus on optimistic and helpful thinking. For example:

- I started off eating well and I will finish my day eating well.

- I'd really like to go to dinner with friends and we'll choose a restaurant with organic, fresh options and I will be so busy talking, I won't overeat.

- This coffee shop makes cappuccino with full-fat milk, which is good for satiety and I could choose to have one.

- I planned to go for a run now and I will do a shorter run that I can fit in.

Another small word that undermines your success is 'try'. When you say, 'I will try to stick to my plan,' or, 'I will try to quit sugar,' you are actually presupposing that not sticking to it or not quitting is acceptable, and when you keep trying and keep not doing what you said you would try to do, your confidence decreases.

Instead, just decide. Decide what you want to do and do it. If you don't want to do it, don't.

If you are used to making decisions that are about pleasing others, you may be uncomfortable with communicating your own needs and saying no. Perhaps you can say no, but you always accompany it with an apology or a sense of doubt – you are responding to what matters to others rather than to you.

Being able to say yes and no is about being in alignment with your values, putting your needs first and accepting that it's OK if others are unhappy with your choices. A genuine yes is said with passion, almost as if you're a child again. The word no is also extremely empowering when you say it confidently, calmly, without any justification. You may even be smiling as you say it. 'No, thank you' may be perfect for you too.

When you are clear on your values and have decided on your boundaries, it is easier to make decisions, easier to say yes and no to the right things. When you choose your language and become aware of your thinking, you will make different choices. NLP has some guiding principles that are also invaluable to making decisions that are best *for you*. There is no such thing as the right decision, just the best decision for you at the time.

These principles are:

- You have all the resources you need to make the changes you want.

- If you want a different outcome, do something differently.

- The person with the most flexible behaviour will have the most success.

In addition to these principles, here are some questions to help you decide on what's best for you:

- If not now, when?

- What specifically is preventing you from doing this now?

- What would you like to have happen?

Remember, choose positive thinking, as negative thinking is a bit like sugar – it's addictive and it sabotages.

 SELF-COACHING ACTIVITY 19:
Agreement frame

For those moments when someone is trying to get you to eat in a way that doesn't fit your new life, learn to use the agreement frame so that you can say no without saying no.

Start your sentence with 'I agree' or similar. Then, instead of 'but', use 'and', which removes the conflict from the sentence. Acknowledge the needs or efforts of the other person and offer an alternative. Do not apologise, justify yourself or make excuses for your choices (eg, don't say 'I'm on a diet').

Here are some examples of agreement framework responses:

- I agree the bread smells amazing, and I would really like some fruit right now, perhaps some blueberries.
- Thank you for being thoughtful and bringing doughnuts. They look so fresh and I am unable to eat one right now as I am full.
- I appreciate your kind invitation and I'll be happy to join you next week.
- While I love chocolate cake and yours looks delicious, I am going to eat the apple I brought with me for lunch.

CASE STUDY: TT puts herself first

TT found clarifying her boundaries and learning to say no helpful when deciding what to do when others in her household were suggesting eating choices that didn't fit in with her plans. She had always eaten what her mother wanted or followed the same diet as her mother, just for convenience's sake, but she now realised that what was right for her mother was not necessarily right for her and that she could choose her own way.

Learning the agreement framework, reframing 'sorry' as 'thank you' and using clean rather than judgemental language, allowed her to communicate her needs clearly with compassion and from an assertive stance, and therefore make more empowered choices. She was ultimately able to let go of worrying about what others were thinking or doing and stay focused on her own journey.

Summary

In this chapter, you have learned how language influences and reflects your thinking, your beliefs, your feelings, your decisions. By changing your language, you can change your thinking habits, build an abundant mindset, break down the go-on-a-diet paradigm and build your confidence so that you can alter your relationship with food.

Positive thinking is not about ignoring mistakes, but about reframing what has happened or is happening to be more optimistic and constructive. When we are critical or judgemental about ourselves, we resist change, because we tend to see it as us needing to be fixed. When we speak kindly to ourselves and have self-compassion, we are more likely to embrace self-improvement.

The unconscious mind needs repetition to create new neural pathways and install a new habit. The more you practise positive thinking, the quicker you will reprogramme your unconscious mind. Two excellent techniques for this are saying affirmations and practising gratitude.

When we negotiate with ourselves, we allow ourselves to change our plan and sabotage our good intentions. When we are clear on our purpose, it is easier to keep our commitment to ourselves and shift our old habits.

Now that you are feeling empowered from decluttering your mind, it is time to build yourself a well-formed outcome, a goal, and create further habits that will support your goal.

PART THREE
BUILD

Are you ready to commit to yourself and your wellbeing with a powerful goal? Now that you have done the critical work of observing how you do food, your habits and patterns, and unravelling the thoughts, beliefs, values and language that have got you to where you are now, it is time to start rebuilding.

First, I will guide you to build yourself an authentic goal, one that is perfect for you. A goal that is congruent with your values and ecological to your body and your world. This section is about identity and purpose, those higher levels of neurological change. When you get clear on who you are and what you want, it impacts more than just you, more than just your body.

It will have consequences for those around you; it will affect your lifestyle, your career, your relationships.

When you are clear on your purpose and your desired outcome, I invite you to go back down the Neurological Levels of Change and consider the fundamental habits you could build to create a sense of wellbeing, to help your mind and body to function at their best. It's a chance to design an empowering daily and weekly routine to help you lose weight naturally. You can then add these routines to your practices developed in Part Two.

FIVE

Design Your Future

How often do you set goals? Knowing who you are and choosing how you want to live your life is integral to success. Getting clarity on what you want and getting into alignment with your true self will give you focus. Otherwise, you get what others decide.

When we go on a diet, we are only focused on losing weight with a target weight in mind or knowing how many pounds we want to lose. Perhaps we want to fit into a dress, be slim for a special occasion – we don't want to be a fat bride – or get 'swimsuit ready'. However, these are all short-term motivations; they have an end date and are focused on a small section of our lives. This means there is no long-term plan, no big vision.

To escape the trap of yo-yo dieting, you need a more holistic goal than losing weight if you truly want to own your body. In this chapter, I guide you through what it is that you truly desire: how you want to feel, your why, what new habits you want to create, what your life will look and feel like when you change.

Identify what is important to you

There is always something drawing on our time and energy, a reason to delay, but if we keep putting our dreams off until tomorrow, they may never happen. We will have even more weight to lose, we could end up ill and we'll have wasted precious days of our life feeling miserable, sluggish and not good enough.

Have you been waiting until the right time to go on your diet? Often, we can't find the motivation to lose weight, but motivation doesn't come from others or outside. We must find it within. It is about uncovering our why, knowing our purpose, so we can build a lifestyle that is totally congruent with ourselves.

If you think you should lose weight because your mum or your dad or your partner or your best friend or your child thinks you should, that is not *your* why. If you think you should go on a diet because you don't look like the women you see in the media, or because you feel guilty when you see the latest ad for yet another dieting miracle, then you won't feel motivated because that's not about you either – those thoughts are about others. If you're telling yourself you don't want to be an overweight wife, a matronly older woman, an exhausted mum or a snappy colleague, that might get you started, but it won't motivate you. You are focusing on what you don't want, not what you do want.

Fear can motivate you briefly too. Perhaps you're afraid of one of the many health risks of weight gain: diabetes, heart disease, a stroke, fatty liver, osteoarthritis, certain cancers or another disease, so you change your diet for a while, but once you forget about that fear in among the realities of your day, you lose sight of your motivation.

The idea of losing weight is not motivational as 'losing' has negative connotations. You don't generally want to lose things in life – money, friends, trust, face – so losing weight doesn't actually *motivate* you.

When you identify your values, your dreams, what matters to you, you can decide what you want – either your present way of life and body or a different way of life and body. When you create a clear vision of the person *you* want to be, not what other people tell you that you should be, you can decide if you want to commit to that change and to being that future self, now.

That woman has a different way of thinking. That woman believes in you. That woman puts wellbeing and joy at the centre of all her decisions. That woman doesn't do crash diets; doesn't deprive herself for several weeks, and then revert to old behaviours that got her to where she was in the first place. That woman designs a lifestyle that nourishes her, that supports her. She is focused on her life rather than her weight.

When you start thinking differently and believing you can, you change you – not just the foods you eat for a few crazy weeks or months. Changing you means taking a risk. It requires courage. When you change, some people may not like the new you. Because the new you puts you first. Your commitment to change needs to be ten or even eleven on a scale of one to ten. Otherwise you won't be able to achieve it – there will be enough doubt to allow chinks in your armour, for lack of success to be an option.

When you hear people tell their success stories, you'll notice they did not force themselves to behave in a particular way. No one can force themselves to behave in a way they don't want to for long and certainly not for the rest of their life! They talk of the vision – the clarity – they had.

If you accept the journey to your dream may not be a straight line, you can plan what to do when you are tempted to go back to old habits, the easy, the familiar. You can even put a plan in place to avoid being in that situation at all. With a plan, you won't need willpower, because you have already decided what you will do. Each time you act in alignment with your plan, you increase your confidence that you can build a new lifestyle. Gradually, your old habits will lose their pull and you will feel empowered.

 SELF-COACHING ACTIVITY 20:
Is it worth it?

To check out whether change is worth it to you, do this short visualisation. Close your eyes and take yourself to a time ten or fifteen years into the future where you have continued eating as you do now, exercising as you do now, living the lifestyle you do now. Notice what you see, hear and feel. What does your body look and feel like? Where are you, who are you with and what are you doing? How do you speak about yourself? What do you say to yourself and what are others saying to you? Notice the impact of your lifestyle and choices on you, your family and your friends. Then slowly come back to the present and open your eyes.

Take a moment to reflect on the impact of continuing to live as you do now and ask yourself if that is what you want to be your legacy, or do you want it to be different? If it's the latter, what do you want to be different?

Now close your eyes again and take yourself to a time ten or fifteen years into the future and create a clear image for when you have changed – what you eat and how you move. Notice how you look and feel different. Notice where you are, who is with you, what they are saying, how you think and behave. What are you able to do? Get a clear picture of that difference, and then come back to now.

Is that difference worth the effort of change? On a scale of one to ten, how committed are you to it?

My story

I woke up one morning, looked in the mirror and realised I had got lost over the years of working so hard, such long hours, and then eating out or ready meals because I was too tired to cook. I had slipped into an 'easy' way of life to focus on my career, yet I felt like I was only surviving. I definitely wasn't thriving. That woman was not me.

Through my goal-setting process, I realised I wanted to have more energy and joy instead of collapsing on the sofa each night and on the weekend. I wanted to be more active and not get in the car even just to go up the road. I wanted a funky and fun wardrobe again instead of the shapeless dark items I'd taken to wearing. I wanted to smile and laugh more instead of being serious all the time. I wanted to have a brighter complexion. I wanted to like having my photo taken when travelling instead of avoiding it. I wanted to enjoy being me. That was my why – to live my life. Not exist alongside a career and accept a body that didn't feel right.

Once I was clear on my motivation, I changed with ease. I could sit with my feelings and ask myself challenging questions. I lost guilt around food choices and made decisions as my future self. No willpower required.

SELF-COACHING ACTIVITY 21:
Your why

Ask yourself what is important to you about losing weight. What will it give you?

Now ask yourself what is important to you about that. Then ask yourself what is important to you about *that*, and so on for your next three replies.

Dig down about five levels – find what is important to you about losing weight, what you really want, and you will find your why.

Focus on what you want

Remember how Oprah said focusing on her weight made her gain weight? That's because we get more of what we focus on. I invite you to be clear on what losing weight will give you so that you can focus on your wellbeing and change your relationship with food instead.

This focus allowed me to:

- Feel at ease around food

- Make food choices with confidence and without guilt

- Eat when hungry and not put it off or eat when triggered

- Stop eating when satisfied rather than when the food was all gone

- Stop weighing myself, but not because I was avoiding it

- Fit into my favourite clothes again
- Feel energised and love life – no more dragging myself out of bed and into action
- Feel balanced and at ease with me
- Smile at myself in the mirror
- Feel confident and in charge of my life
- Achieve other goals in my life more easily

Creating a well-formed outcome is not like the goal when you join a slimming club to lose X% of your body weight and the group leader tells you how many pounds or kilogrammes that is. This is about setting a goal that's meaningful to you; that will motivate and focus you so you're not fighting willpower; that focuses on the feeling you will experience, a future you're committed to.

A well-formed outcome is holistic and embraces your whole life. Completing a wheel of wellbeing allows you to see where you are out of balance in your life and can direct you to where you could most benefit from making change. It can also direct your mind to the areas in your life that are causing your struggle with weight gain. Importantly, it will make clear where you are doing well in your life, what gives you strength.

A well-formed outcome focuses on what you will gain rather than what you will lose. In NLP, we call this *towards* thinking. If you focus your unconscious mind on what you want more of, it will work in the background, helping you achieve it. If you focus on being 'not fat' or 'not frumpy' – what you don't like and what NLP calls *away* thinking – your unconscious mind will give you more of that. Logically, then, for success, you need to direct your brain towards what you *do* want.

 SELF-COACHING ACTIVITY 22:
Wheel of wellbeing

Draw a circle and divide it into eight pieces. Each piece represents an area of your life. The most commonly used categories are physical, emotional, intellectual, social, spiritual, environmental, financial and occupational. You could choose other categories, such as family or one that reflects the pain point in your relationship with food right now.

For each category, rate where you feel you are from one to ten, where one is not doing at all well and ten is awesome. Take a moment to reflect on patterns in your wheel, what changes you may wish to make and how making those changes could translate into any goal you set yourself.

 SELF-COACHING ACTIVITY 23:
Focus on what you want

A good place to start this activity is by writing down what it is you have now that you don't want, and then writing down what you want instead, what that would look like in the new you. For example:

- Tired might become rested and energised.
- Fat could be toned and slender.
- Stressed may be calm and organised.
- Having no time could become making time for me.
- Critical of myself could be proud and kind to myself.

Create a clear vision

Bring back to mind the vision of your future when you changed (Self-coaching Activity 20). This section will help you build on that. Why? Because when you have a clear vision of your future, you can make more empowered decisions for yourself. When you have a clear vision, you make your life happen rather than it happening to you.

You can't control what others do, but you can decide with more clarity what is best for you. When you know who you will be in ten years' time, you can act now in ways that will ensure you get to be that person.

Once you get specific about who you want to be, you will notice it encompasses all areas of your life. You are more than your weight. When you start looking at the big picture – your lifestyle, what really matters – you will become clear on who you are: what you do, think, believe, look like; where you are; how you feel and behave; who you are with. You will notice it's not about how hungry you can make yourself, or how exhausted you can get with a brand-new fitness regime, or how much to set aside for gym membership that you promise yourself you'll use this time, or the monthly cost of a diet plan.

Creating a clearly visualised, compelling and personally meaningful goal that feels really empowering releases dopamine. Dopamine is the most powerful neurotransmitter and is frequently referred to as the reward chemical. We produce it when we're anticipating something amazing, and then actually having it. It is also the chemical that is our motivator to get out there and achieve our goals. Our brain naturally seeks dopamine, so adding mini goals and rewards to your well-formed outcome will serve you well.

Your unconscious mind does not know the difference between what's imagined and what is real, so the more you visualise and rehearse your future you, the more your unconscious mind can support you to achieve it. In addition to doing Self-coaching Activity 24, you could create a vision board of what your life will be like. If you pin it up, you will keep your vision clearly in the forefront of your mind.

On your vision board, take care to avoid pictures of 'perfect' people so you don't end up comparing yourself to others. All our bodies are different and this is not about how you look, but about how you feel. Choose images that represent choices you will make, such as:

- Food that you will eat to feel better

- Food you could grow or pictures of prettily arranged food

- Activities you will do to build flexibility and lift your energy

- Activities that inspire you

- Clothing styles and colours that give you confidence

- Self-care images

- Inspiring quotes

 SELF-COACHING ACTIVITY 24:
Visualise your future

To start crafting your goal, close your eyes and hold in your mind an image of what you ultimately want to achieve and that moment when you are living that lifetime goal. This is best done standing tall, with feet slightly apart and an open and clear chest. Notice:

- Where you are
- When it is
- What you're wearing
- What you're thinking

- What you're feeling
- What you believe about yourself and the world
- What changes you have made to your lifestyle to get here
- What inspires you and energises you

Step forward and put yourself in the picture. Feel the confidence that you have at this time. See, hear and feel very clearly that moment, making the picture perfect for you, as if you have achieved it already.

You could create an NLP anchor of this moment to inspire you by pressing your right thumb with your left hand when the image is at its peak. You can revisit this inspiring moment by using your anchor, pressing your right thumb, every day.

Write your well-formed outcome

Did you know that writing things down supports your unconscious mind too?[51] A well-formed outcome is written with the date you've imagined achieving it in the present tense as if you have achieved it already. It should also be stated using positive language.

Again, this is about what you are aiming towards rather than what you don't want to be, feel or have, what you want to get away from. Remember, don't say 'not fat' as the mind can only process the word 'fat'. Instead, give your mind clues as to what 'not fat' means for you. Use your visualisation and be specific as to the benefits and the transformation you've achieved. Be specific about your habits that got you there.

You may want to avoid stating what you weigh in your visualisation. Focus on how you are feeling and what you are thinking and doing. You may even want to avoid stating what size clothes you are wearing, especially if that triggers negative feelings for you. Focus on the *type* of clothes you're wearing and how they fit and feel instead.

Ensure the date you choose gives you a reasonable timeframe if you were to make small changes to your routines and habits. Remember, this is a long-term strategy that will benefit your wellbeing, and your body weight will change slowly. Choose a date that feels right for you – not what you think you should achieve because that's what others have managed or what someone has told you is possible. Have in mind a safe and sustainable change.

 SELF-COACHING ACTIVITY 25:
Your goal

Write out your well-formed outcome on a piece of card and tuck it in your journal or planner or wallet. Somewhere safe where you can see it often:

On [date] I am [place]. I am wearing..., I feel..., I believe..., I think..., I have... [list the changes you have made].

Break it down

Are you ready to get even more specific? You can use your visualisation to get more clarity on how to achieve your goal: steps, resources, barriers, how to measure and celebrate your progress.

First, identify the steps you need to take. Look back from when you have achieved your goal. Notice the steps you took to get there and that there is more than one way to achieve your goal. Identify any small changes you could make and decide what order you will take the steps in and when you will take them. Do not change everything at once as that will overwhelm you and sabotage your outcome. Build on your successes one at a time. Identify the first step you will take and know that you will be flexible around the other small steps as you make sustainable progress towards your goal.

Next, it is important to identify any resources you need to achieve your goal: skills, support, a role model. A role model is not someone who has told you about a diet plan they have followed to lose weight, but someone who has successfully changed their lifestyle. Study what specifically they have done differently.

Resources could also include:

- Taking a nutrition course or getting the support of a nutritionist.

- Joining a group of positive-minded people intent on achieving their goal or a group doing something you enjoy.

- Seeking an accountability buddy or a coach – your cheerleader and advocate, someone who's non-judgemental and challenges your thinking.

Support aside, your goal should be achievable by you alone as you cannot control the behaviour of others around you. In fact, other people could be a barrier to your success.

What other potential barriers could you identify? A barrier often cited is 'lack of willpower'. With your perfectly crafted goal, you won't need to rely on power of will, but if you break the phrase down – the will to do what specifically – it will help you reflect on possible barriers from your past that you could over-come or address. For me, it was not having the will to starve myself while doing a job that demanded my full attention, the will to cook at the end of the long day, the will to say no, the will to make my lunch for the next day.

Some other barriers that clients have identified are:

- The size of their plates

- A co-habitant who refuses to eat healthily

- Working shifts

- Keeping treats in the house for others

- Frequent holidays
- Socialising and drinking often
- Disliking vegetables
- An addiction to sugar

Another important element to the detail is a system to measure and celebrate your progress. Focusing on progress rather than achievement is about looking at where you have moved from rather than seeing the gap between where you are now and where you want to get to. This avoids the thought 'I've got so far to go' or 'I haven't achieved my goal', which can make you feel like giving up or create the state of despair when you haven't lost weight one week.

There are many ways to acknowledge progress in changing your relationship with food; it's not just about weight loss. Get creative! Perhaps use a habit tracker to record how much water you drink, how much movement you do, what foods you add to your diet, how often you say your affirmation or gratitudes, how long you sleep, how well you feel.

Celebration and rewards work in the same way as gratitude, rewiring our brain, firing our neural pathways for dopamine, which makes us feel good. We are programmed to seek rewards. If we want to succeed at our goal, creating rewards related to our goal and scheduling regular celebrations in our planner will boost our motivation and keep us optimistic. Our brain is not programmed to celebrate loss, so we need to reward ourselves for the actual progress we have made – the changes we have created – rather than the weight we have lost.

Focusing on your small wins makes you feel proud and builds confidence. Small changes have great impact over time. The more you reflect on and acknowledge what you have achieved, the more your confidence builds and propels you towards your goal. It's a great idea to record your successes, perhaps in a video diary, on Post-its, in your journal, on scraps of paper stored in a jar. This gives you something to go back to if you doubt yourself because progress and change can be so gradual, you may not notice how what you have achieved is adding up.

If you are a perfectionist, learning to celebrate small wins prevents self-sabotage. Applying the Pareto Principle (see Chapter 7) where you accept that 80% of what you intended is good enough can also help prevent self-sabotage.

Choose some rewards that don't involve food to break that pattern. When you do choose food or drink rewards from the occasional or rarely levels of your pyramid, remember all calories are not equal. For example, wine. Research suggests that the occasional glass of red wine is good for you because of its powerful antioxidants, anti-inflammatory properties, and glucose metabolism and lipid-regulating effects.[52]

Wine has residual sugar – it is not added sugar. Red wine has a lower sugar content than rosé or white wine, of which dry wine has a lower sugar content than sweeter wine.[53] Counterintuitively, the less sugar the wine contains, the higher its calories because it has a higher alcohol content, and alcohol has more calories per gram than sugars (carbohydrates). A glass of sparkling wine is the lowest calorie option and choosing a dry version would reduce the sugar content. Vodka is also popular as a reward, because it has the lowest number of calories of any alcohol and no sugars.[54] However, any mixer that is added will change that. Even choosing light or sugar-free mixer options is not risk-free. Choosing any alcohol is about balance, as it affects how your body metabolises fats and sugars and it increases appetite.[55]

My story

I reframed my habitual and mindless drinking of alcohol each evening as I worked. I saw the wine as a reward for a long day and thought I needed it to keep me going.

A turning point for me was when I chose instead to mark the weekend by drinking alcohol only on Friday or Saturday night as a celebration that this was my time. I also chose to stop after one or two glasses of wine each evening to avoid binge drinking. Far from making me feel deprived as I thought it would, it made the wine that I did choose to drink much more enjoyable and my weekends even more special.

SELF-COACHING ACTIVITY 26:
Your goal plan

Create a plan for your goal. This needs to include:

- The steps necessary to get there with dates (your mini milestones).
- The first step you will take.
- The resources you have already and those you need.
- The barriers you may come up against.
- How and when you will celebrate your progress.

Identify possible secondary gain

How come you don't have it already? This is an important question to ask to succeed at your goal. Reflecting more deeply on what has prevented you from achieving your goal in the past will help you identify the barriers to success we looked at earlier and allow you to overcome them.

Often, your barriers are not obvious. When you can't seem to achieve a goal you are telling yourself you want, there is something that your perceived problem is giving you that you're not willing to give up. In NLP, we call this secondary gain.

Secondary gain is unconscious or conscious beliefs or values that are preventing us from making changes as we are benefiting from the problem in some way. Sometimes, we're aware of our secondary gain on some level, but we may be afraid to unravel what is going on or ashamed about how being overweight is benefiting us. When we are in this place of protection, we can't grow.

Possible examples of secondary gain are:

- You're paid attention when you are overweight, both in positive and negative ways. People talk about you, they care about you and may want to help you, finding solutions for you.

- Your weight or talking about losing weight has become integral to your identity and you are in a community of like-minded women and don't want to let that go.

- You use food to comfort yourself, to relax or to fit in.

- You're scared to damage a relationship by eating differently to your spouse, partner or family or changing your body.

- You experienced feeling unsafe when you were slimmer and you protect yourself by being larger.

SELF-COACHING ACTIVITY 27:
Secondary gain

Consider these questions to access your thinking on a deeper level and uncover what you're hiding from.

Write down your problem first so that you can explore it with these prompts and allow your unconscious mind to generate a solution.

- What will you gain or lose if you achieve your goal?
- What will others gain or lose if you achieve your goal?
- What will happen if you achieve your goal?
- What won't happen if you achieve your goal?
- What will happen if you don't achieve your goal?
- What won't happen if you don't achieve your goal?

Be that person now

Does your goal excite you? Does it motivate you to be that person right now?

Often, we put off living life until we lose weight. Perhaps you even have a mental to-do list for 'When I lose weight' or have stopped yourself doing something or turned down an invitation in the past because you 'need to lose weight first'.

It's time to decide to think slim now. Notice the difference if you appreciate what is right about your body. When you stand tall with your feet apart, breathe in and push your breath low, and hold your core muscles tight, you feel more confident. Make your decisions from this place.

Act as if you are your future self already and make decisions as that person. Often, even when we have lost weight, we still don't think like the slim person we have become. We hold ourselves back, we continue to act as we were before because we haven't changed our beliefs, our thoughts, our values or our identity. This means we put back on the weight we have lost.

To be your future self now, refer back to Dilts's Neurological Levels of Change model in Chapter 2. This time, start at the top. Once you are clear on your purpose and your why, which we covered at the beginning of this chapter, your identity will also be clear. You can then identify what beliefs empower you and what thoughts are helpful to this you. Then you learn the skills you need, alter how you behave and make changes to your environment to support you and your ability to succeed now. When you decide who you are and live those thinking habits now, you will make more empowered choices. You will keep to your plans, dress with confidence and participate in activities.

Don't overthink it. Don't waste your time and energy wondering about what others may be thinking about you and your choices. Just be true to you.

As you work towards and achieve your goal, notice if there are other changes you can make that will support you further. Keep an eye on your habits and make sure they are empowering you and not sabotaging you.

Summary

In this chapter, we have examined what it is that you truly desire: how you want to feel, your why, what new habits you want to create, what your life will look and feel like when you change.

Often, we can't find the motivation to lose weight, but motivation doesn't come from others or outside. We have to find it within ourselves. It is about uncovering our why, knowing our purpose, so we can build a lifestyle that is totally congruent with ourselves.

To find our why, we need to dig deep and uncover what it is we truly want for our whole selves. This chapter has taken you through several techniques to set your unconscious mind on the right path to get you exactly where you do want to be, not where you don't want to be. Once you are living your best life, you will lose weight naturally because you will be enjoying all the benefits of being active and nourished, of self-care. No willpower required.

In the next chapter, we will look at fundamental habits you could build to create a daily and weekly routine that will support your wellbeing and your goal. We are going back down the levels in Dilts's Neurological Levels of Change model.

SIX
Thrive, Not Survive

Do you sometimes feel like Superwoman with a busy, demanding job and running an efficient home? You may have been told you can have it all, but really, you're just juggling a myriad of responsibilities. If you have developed the narrative that you are time poor, you probably choose the quickest and most convenient way to get everything done.

This narrative is likely to have affected your daily routines and your relationship with food. How much you eat and sleep, what you eat and do, when you eat, rest and exercise, where and with whom you eat and move. Because you're supposed to make sure you look good too, you've adopted the go-on-a-diet paradigm.

Retaining a sense of wellbeing and a more consistent body size and shape is about creating a new lifestyle full of healthy habits that will support your energy needs. Adopting intentional habits is transformational: it can empower you to stop merely surviving and instead truly flourish.

Your eating diary will show you the habits you have in your life that affect your eating patterns, so will help you identify what habits are unhelpful and which ones would be useful to you to build or maintain. Using your diary along with this chapter, you will identify potential new habits to create a lifestyle to maintain a healthy body weight, feel more balanced and successful.

I will guide you through these areas:

- Managing your time and priorities around food and eating
- Getting enough sleep
- Reducing stress

How to create new habits

When you look at your eating habits diary, how much of your eating is unconscious? Unless you're trying to eat with chopsticks for the first time, you're eating something new or you're on a date and feeling self-conscious, much of your eating is unconscious. There may even be times when you've finished your food, but can't remember eating it, let alone enjoying it.

Perhaps you go to the goody drawer and chose something to eat even when you're not really hungry, or you grab something sweet while you're watching the TV even though you've eaten, or pour a glass of wine while cooking, or find yourself planning what you're going to eat as you travel home. Your unconscious mind stores your memories of food: when you learned not to like a food or that moment when you created a fond memory of a food that prompts a longing now, even though when you actually eat it, it doesn't give you that feeling you thought you would get.

You may have heard the saying 'neurons that fire together, wire together'. This expression, paraphrased from work done by neuropsychologist Donald Hebb in 1949,[56] beautifully describes how our brain builds habits consciously and unconsciously through repetition.

For example, we may teach ourselves to eat at a particular time – we learn to eat lunch at 1pm because that's the break time that's been assigned to us in our workplace. We may inadvertently teach ourselves to eat chocolate when we watch TV because we repeat the behaviour. Each behaviour we create as a habit has a cue, a trigger, that tells us it's time to do our habit – the position of the hands on the clock or the act of sitting down to watch the TV in the same seat reminds us to eat, whether we are hungry or not.

We may have habits that combine to sabotage us. For example, I had a habit of putting things off until later, and that showed up as leaving making my breakfast and lunch until the morning as I was too tired to be bothered at night, and then snoozing the alarm for just five more minutes rather than getting up in good time. This meant in the morning, I was too rushed to prepare my meals after all, so I ended up grabbing breakfast and lunch on the go.

To change your habits, you have to bring them into your conscious awareness. The easiest way to break a habit is by intervening before it starts, which is why in your eating diary introduced in Chapter 2, you are asked to identify the triggers to your eating. When you slow down and observe how you do your habit, then you can work out where you can intervene.

According to neuroscientist Jill Bolte Taylor, we are on autopilot for ninety seconds, and after that, we 'either consciously or unconsciously choose to rethink the thought that triggered the emotion circuit to run'.[57] That means there is a ninety-second chemical process that happens in the body, and after that has finished, we are choosing to stay in the loop we are in.

For example, you feel stressed, which has triggered a craving for chocolate. The emotional chemicals take ninety seconds to flush through your body, and then it is up to you whether you continue with the craving or distract yourself.

Focusing on our breathing calms our emotional (limbic) brain, allowing our thinking (prefrontal cortex) brain to kick in. It allows us to assess what we're feeling and let those emotions wash over us before we formulate a response. This response, like all behaviour changes, requires practice to put it on autopilot and alter our long-term behaviour.

Longer term, it is possible to interrupt a pattern by removing the trigger. For example, by sitting in a different chair when you watch TV, removing negative people from your circle, ordering groceries online.

Building a new habit is easier than breaking an old habit. When you link your new habit to an existing habit that is part of your routine or to a particular time, it is easier to form and on average, it takes fifty-nine days to put it on autopilot.[58] How long it takes exactly will depend on how entrenched any unwanted habit is that interferes, your level of commitment to your new habit, your self-perception and the stories you are telling yourself.

As you read this chapter, focus on building one habit at a time or on linked habits, for example, your morning and evening routine together, or several aspects to an evening wind-down routine. Your unconscious mind needs repetition to put a habit on autopilot. Make small sustainable changes one at a time and gradually build your habits.

Build routines to manage your wellbeing

What self-care do you have as part of your routine? Self-care is often promoted as an add-on and can feel like something else to feel guilty about, something else you don't have time to do. In this section, I look at integrating self-care into your daily routine, the key to creating an empowering lifestyle.

A routine is about how you spend your time on any given day or in any given week, month or year. It is a collection of habits that you do on a regular basis. You may have routines and habits for work and home, routines and habits for mornings and evenings, week-days and weekends, winter and summer.

A key component of your routine is your sleep pattern. Lack of sleep is associated with numerous life-changing conditions: obesity, type 2 diabetes, stress, depression, dementia, cancer, heart disease, irritable bowel syndrome, and other chronic health conditions.[59] It produces cortisol, which causes weight gain and impaired brain function and immune system.

Lack of sleep makes you feel hungry. If you don't get enough sleep, your body doesn't produce your hunger moderating hormones in the right proportion.

The main two are ghrelin and leptin: ghrelin signals hunger and leptin suppresses hunger and signals that you are full. When they are upside down, it leaves you feeling hungry and unable to control your cravings.

When we're tired, we crave fats, carbohydrates and sugar to give us energy and get rid of the brain fog. A meta-analysis of research suggests we consume on average 385 extra calories a day when we don't get enough sleep.[60] If we are permanently sleep deprived, we end up in that vicious cycle of dieting to head off the weight gain – if we have the energy – oblivious to the fact that a few hours more sleep a night would make us feel better and solve our problems.

To perform at our best, be healthy and manage our weight, an adult generally needs seven to nine hours' sleep a night.[61] An evening routine can help you wind down, go to bed earlier and improve your sleep quality. This routine could include:

- Avoiding blue light from your phone, computer or TV for an hour before sleep as it prevents the release of melatonin, the hormone that helps you sleep

- Using an app to remind you to go to bed

- Writing your to-do list for the next day so you can switch off

- Keeping a gratitude journal to feel positive as you doze off

- Soaking in a bath

- Reading a relaxing book

- Smelling relaxing essential oils, like lavender

- Listening to a sleep meditation

- Visualising a time when you fell asleep easily

This can be complemented with a morning routine to support you to maintain balanced eating during the day. A possible morning routine could include:

- Drinking water

- Stretching and moving

- Smelling uplifting essential oils (like citrus)

- Setting your intention for the day

- Journaling

- Re-reading your gratitudes from the night before

- Using your goal anchor

- Taking an invigorating cold shower

Creating a movement routine is also important for wellbeing. You may be averse to exercise; perhaps you've grown up hating it, so you may want to reframe it as 'movement' because movement makes us feel better physically and emotionally. The good news is what you eat is more important than exercise when it comes to losing weight.[62] For example, if you walk or run 10 miles a day four times a week, you could lose a pound a week, and that exercise level would also make you more hungry.[63] However, although diet is more effective than exercise for losing weight, a combination of diet and movement is the most balanced way to feel well and maintain a strong body.

Movement not only allows your body to be more supple, build more bone and muscle strength and feel energised, it also helps you de-stress. It lifts your mood, which supports you to make more helpful eating choices; it boosts serotonin and endorphins, and it can be used to trigger dopamine to motivate you. It also protects your brain. Exercising while dieting helps you maintain muscle mass as you lose fat.[64]

Choose movement you may enjoy rather than something you think you should do; consider if individual, group and organised or independent activity is best for you. Choose an activity that gives you an outcome you desire. Start small and do some movement every day, and build on that. If you do it at the same time every day, it's easier to build the habit. Focus on making progress rather than being perfect.

Here are some examples you may like to consider:

- A brisk walk is really uplifting and allows your brain to get creative; it can be done anywhere and costs nothing.

- A team sport like netball provides community and support.

- Swimming supports muscles if you haven't done any exercise in years.

- Yoga combines exercise with meditation.

- Weightlifting builds muscle mass and bone density and you can use items around the house.

- Dancing lifts the mood and can be done alone at home or at a class.

- Skating can be inline, roller disco or on ice, solo or with friends.

- Skipping doesn't take long to raise your cardio rate and is easy to build progress.

- Hula-hooping improves core muscle strength and balance for a relatively low equipment cost.

- You can consider less common games like dodgeball, underwater hockey, Quidditch, Frisbee.

 SELF-COACHING ACTIVITY 28:
Create your empowering routines

Design an evening routine that will set you up for a good night's sleep and a morning routine for a focused day. Notice from your eating diary where movement would fit well to provide energy in your day so that you will get maximum benefit, as well as what, when and where will be easiest to fit into your daily and weekly routine.

SELF-COACHING ACTIVITY 29:
Installing a routine

Use this New Behaviour Generator technique to install your morning or evening or movement routine in your unconscious mind, as it allows you to rehearse the behaviour so that your brain thinks you already do it. Ensure you follow the eye movements.

Look down to your left and ask yourself, 'What do I want to do differently?' Focus on what will help you eat more healthily or have more energy.

Then ask, 'What would that look like?' as you turn your eyes to look up to the right. See yourself doing the new behaviour and notice how it affects you.

Next, look down to the right and step into the experience, feeling it and doing it. Notice what feels right and how you can adjust your idea.

Repeat the cycle at least three times, refining it as you go. The more times you rehearse, the more your unconscious mind gets to practise your new habit.

My story

For me, Superwoman was most definitely the issue. I was so busy that I cut out sleep to get what I needed to done. For years, I worked late into the night or into the small hours, sometimes even going without any sleep at all. Then I'd try to catch up on the weekend and in school holidays.

When I learned that our sleep debt cannot be corrected by weekend lie-ins and that we are better off with regular sleeping patterns, I decided I had to change. My biggest fear is dementia, a recognised risk of sleep deprivation. Through coaching, I worked out that I am task driven, and hence I would always be thinking, 'I'll just do this', 'I'll just do that'. That's why, before I knew it, it would be silly o'clock and I had no time to sleep.

Using the NLP Swish technique, which we'll cover in Self-coaching Activity 34 in Chapter 7, I changed my thought pattern to, 'No, it's time to sleep now', which has helped me to go to bed earlier. I also created a relaxation anchor, visualising myself on the beach and floating in the sea to induce a relaxed state once I was in bed. I used the New Behaviour Generator in Self-coaching Activity 29 to make sure I would get up when my alarm went off rather than keep snoozing it. It took me a year or so to start to feel better and get my circadian rhythms back into balance and pay off my sleep debt.

I worked out that I hate exercise because I can't stand sweating or being out of breath. Also, because I don't like it, I'd see exercise as getting in the way of my day and doing things. For these reasons, I chose skipping, walking and Pilates. Skipping I could do in short bursts and build it up so I wouldn't get too out of breath, and it doesn't take long. Walking gets me out of an energy slump and helps my brain come up with creative ideas by the time I get back. Pilates helps me build core strength and balance.

Manage your stress

Is stress so much part of your day that you don't notice it? Are you so stressed you're at the point of burnout?

Overwork and overwhelm can lead to us being overweight. When we are stressed, our body releases the hormone cortisol as part of our fight or flight response. Stress can also affect our ability to sleep, which then adds more cortisol to our system, as discussed above.

Cortisol changes the way that our body metabolises glucose and how much energy our muscles burn.[65] Constant release of cortisol may increase our risk of developing insulin resistance. It raises our blood sugar, alters our appetite, reduces our ability to burn fat and increases the rate at which we store fat, especially abdominal visceral fat, putting us at risk of obesity.

While eustress – positive short-term stress related to achieving a goal – may cause a loss in appetite, long-term or chronic stress can increase your hunger. Chronic stress results in higher insulin levels, which means your blood sugar levels drop, causing you to crave sugary, fatty foods. Instead of the healthy foods you would usually eat, you are likely to start eating comfort foods. The more stress you are under, and the longer you are under that stress, the more severe your symptoms are likely to be.

Some possible symptoms of stress are:

- Permanent low energy
- Weight gain, especially on the waistline and abdominal area
- Needing caffeine to keep going
- Cravings for sugary, fatty or salty foods
- Energy crash in mid-afternoon and a second wind in the evening
- Racing mind preventing you from focusing and sleeping
- Difficulty sleeping, and then getting up in the morning
- Mood changes and feeling unmotivated, depressed or anxious

The only way to truly resolve stress is to address its source. Stress can come from a range of sources:

- Physical – over-exercising, over-dieting, not sleeping, working long hours
- Social – peer pressure, relationship breakdown, bullying
- Emotional – draining work, post-traumatic stress disorder, worry about deadlines or performance, financial difficulties, grief

- Environmental – lack of fresh air, too much noise and exposure to electronic devices

- Health – chronic conditions, hormones, poor nutrition, depression

Keeping to a strict diet can be stressful because you worry about the number of calories and what you can eat,[66] and if you have been dieting for an extended period, you are at risk of creating metabolic damage,[67] as well as increasing cortisol, which may further reduce your metabolism. Over-exercising may also cause release of cortisol, which means your belly fat will not reduce.[68] Balance is key.

Here are some effective ways to reduce your stress levels:

- Stop what you are doing, acknowledge your stress and breathe. Breathe out for longer than you breathe in and push your breathing down to your belly. You can say to yourself 'rest and digest' (the opposite system of fight or flight) as you breathe in and out.

- Go for a walk to change your environment and shift your thinking. Even ten minutes can improve your resilience.

- Add movement to your routine to relieve stress. Make sure it leaves you revitalised, not tired.

- Reframe the situation – put yourself outside of your situation and advise yourself. Look for what you can change or re-prioritise.

- Adopt a visualisation exercise, such as putting yourself in a bubble of a calming colour, or imagining the person causing you stress as a cartoon character. Imagine the situation solved.

- Add an affirmation to promote focus and calm to your daily routine.

- Do something creative or listen to your favourite music.

- Surround yourself with positive people and laughter.

- Avoid restrictive diets and instead focus on foods that will help you lose weight by giving you energy.

 SELF-COACHING ACTIVITY 30:
Your stress strategy

To identify your stress strategy, ask yourself:

- How do I know I'm stressed?
- What is my trigger?
- What is my self-talk?
- What behaviours do I do when stressed and in what order? Are there are any alternatives?
- How do I know it's time to stop?

With that knowledge, create a plan to interrupt your stress strategy, either *before* it starts or *during* it as it plays out. Before is the more powerful as you weaken the wiring for the stress habit to be triggered.

My story

I know I am stressed when I find myself looking for food 'to settle myself' so that I can work. Usually, I am at my desk, finding work hard and telling myself that I don't have enough time or to stop procrastinating. I'm feeling overwhelmed by a big or urgent project or a to-do list that goes on forever.

My before strategy is to limit and prioritise my to-do list (seven key things) and chunk projects into actions. Should I overlook those critical steps, my during strategy when I find myself at the food cupboard, is to stop, lower my breathing, tell myself that there is always time and I can just do a bit, laugh, grab a cup of water and start the task. Sometimes, I may go outside or do something different for a while.

Plan your eating

Do you like to plan, or would you rather wing it? Do you plan your work and ignore your personal life? The trouble with the term 'eating plan' is that it has become loaded with dieting connotations, yet the more you plan your eating, the easier it is to achieve your goal. When you plan, it allows you to foresee issues that may sabotage you. Creating an eating routine helps build healthy habits and reduces the need to decide what to eat.

An eating routine allows you to:

- Go straight to the cupboard and fridge to get out what you need, thus preventing the 'searching for something to eat' scenario

- Eat the same size portion each day, avoiding deciding how much you want or how hungry you are, which may trigger loophole thinking or a gradual increase in portion size

- Know what food you will buy and where you're going in the supermarket, so you won't be at risk of temptation by wandering up and down the aisles

- Speed up the food preparation process as less thinking is required

- Avoid wondering what you're in the mood for, which reduces the risk of choosing less nutritious foods

Decide what you will eat. Plan your meals for the week, keep them simple and natural, and get the ingredients to make them happen. Aim for straightforward meals that you can prepare quickly. Rather than going to the supermarket, you may decide to shop online so you are not tempted to buy foods not on your list.

Put your plan of meals and the recipes in a highly visible place in the kitchen to keep you focused. Identify a range of breakfasts and lunches for each day ready to take with you in the mornings, so you don't end up having to eat what's available at work.

Know where your stress points are in the week and prepare in advance so you can avoid the excuse of 'I don't have time to cook'. Even plan for a ready meal so you don't end up thinking 'I'll just stop and get a takeaway tonight and start again tomorrow' or 'I'll buy a ready meal on the way home'. That way, you avoid being in the supermarket in a hurry when you are hungry and at risk of buying unhelpful foods, which then triggers failure thinking.

Decide where you will eat. Create a designated place to eat each of your meals, or at least move away from where you are working or watching the TV. Consider laying the table to celebrate this vital nourishing act. Make it new by using different utensils, sitting in a different seat and choosing a different – preferably smaller – plate.

Decide when you will eat. One way to optimise your eating rhythms is by choosing to eat within a certain period each day. From a mindset point of view, this is about reducing the time you focus on food. From a physical point of view, your circadian rhythms control the presence of insulin and melatonin, which affect your body's ability to digest, absorb and metabolise food, and these are more effective earlier in the day.[69] Decide what time the kitchen is going to open and close so you can create a consistent eating rhythm.

Evidence suggests that creating an overnight fasting period optimises brain function, energy metabolism and healthy signalling of metabolic hormones.[70] Recent research on the impact of eating four hours later shows it makes a significant difference to our leptin levels, so our satiety hormone drops over twenty-four hours.[71] Eating late also means we burn calories more slowly and it negatively impacts the way we store fat.[72] What also seems to be true is when we eat later, we eat a higher total number of calories, that our food choices at that time are associated with weight gain.[73]

If you find yourself being attracted to eating something after the kitchen has closed for the night, use one of your alternative activities to soothe the emotion that is driving your desire to eat. Review your trigger and check that you have eaten enough nourishing foods through the day.

CASE STUDY: Sarah's preparation routine

A client, Sarah, found that she would end up choosing unhealthy foods in the canteen at work when she was tired on a long shift. She decided she could eat more nutritiously if she took her own food, which required changing some other habits. She chose to do her grocery shopping after she had eaten so that she only bought foods that were on her list rather than what grabbed her attention in the store. Then, she was able to keep to her plan and avoid poor choices triggered by being over-hungry and exhausted.

 SELF-COACHING ACTIVITY 31: Eating routines

Get out your food diary and start working out what would be an empowering eating routine for you. Look at your unhelpful triggers and decide what would help you avoid those scenarios. To get clarity on what to do, ask yourself these questions about both the old and the new habit:

- What has to happen for that to happen?
- What has to happen before that?

Summary

In this chapter, we have explored the significance of what we do every day. We have identified the importance of sleep and looked at effective ways to ensure we start every day rested after a good night's sleep. Movement is also essential to our wellbeing and ability to perform at our best, but we need to beware of taking on an activity because we feel we should, as this is unsustainable, or over-exercising.

We then analysed our stress strategy and came up with empowering routines and habits to combat chronic stress. Finally, we looked at how an eating plan can help us to achieve our goal, build healthy habits and reduce the need to decide what to eat.

In the next section, Part Four, we will look at how to manage and monitor change over time, as well as those events and occasions that in the past may have sabotaged us.

PART FOUR
MAINTAIN

How many times have you celebrated losing weight only to go back to old habits and put the weight on again? Maintaining weight loss and living our new identity is a bigger challenge even than losing the weight because it takes a permanent change in the way we think, and if we are not careful, we can easily slide.

The more motivated we are to be our best selves, the easier the work of change. Our slimmer, stronger, fitter identity and lifestyle need to be more attractive and worthwhile to us than the easier route of keeping doing what we have always done. When we take a sustainable approach of small changes at a time and do the inner work to support the change, then it is more likely to last.

Making conscious decisions that embrace the power of the unconscious mind allows you to change your relationship with food. When you develop a more intuitive way to eat, you function from an empowered state. In Part Four, we will explore the habits of an empowered eater and what to look out for over time.

SEVEN

Embrace Empowered Eating

What if you paid more attention to the needs of your body than the impulses of your mind? A restrictive diet may allow you to lose weight, but as we've discovered, it doesn't build a helpful relationship with food and it is not sustainable. It is your daily diet, your daily habits, that affects your physical and mental wellbeing, and your ability to maintain weight loss.

In this chapter, we will continue to build a lifestyle that is perfect for you and will support you to create your ideal eating plan and allow you to keep your weight off. Instead of following other people's rules, it's time to decide on your own rules for living and eating. You know what makes you feel good, and it is not following what has worked for other people. It is not overindulging yourself all the time.

I invite you to learn a few more tools and build habits to become an intuitive and empowered eater.

Listen to your body

Do you feel like you've been battling with your body most of your life? From years of yo-yo dieting, you have probably come to believe that you don't know how to eat to maintain a healthy weight and body. Once you focus on creating a lifestyle that gives you energy and start to listen to the wisdom of your body, you will learn to trust yourself again, and from there you can gradually build the perfect diet for you.

As you have read this book and done the exercises, you have developed your awareness of yourself and your environment. You have started to make conscious what you have been doing unconsciously, to be more conscious of the impact of your choices.

If you have been eating on the go, in a hurry, while you do something else, inhaling your food, then learning to eat more mindfully will support you to eat more intuitively. Research suggests it may also help with food cravings, binge eating, triggered eating and emotional eating.[74]

When you are mindful in your eating, you are intentional about what, where and how you eat, and you choose food for its quality and what it gives you. You use your senses to experience and enjoy your food and pay attention to your body as you eat. Eating more consciously in this way encourages you to eat slowly and choose food that is satisfying and nourishing.

OLD HABIT	NEW HABIT
✘ Eat on the go	✓ Create an eating area
✘ Eat while doing something else	✓ Give eating your full focus
✘ Inhale your food	✓ Eat slowly and appreciatively
✘ Eat when you're triggered	✓ Eat when you have hunger pangs
✘ Eat until your plate is empty, even when full, to please others, from habit, FOMO	✓ Stop eating when you're satisfied
✘ Eat mainly convenient, fast, processed food	✓ Cook with ethical, local, fresh food, focusing on brain, gut and heart health

Shift from unconscious to conscious eating

Eating quickly, or mindless eating, leads to poor digestion, poor nutrition, increased weight gain and lower satisfaction with our food. It may cause us to overeat as the body does not have a chance to register what we have eaten.

Fast eaters are up to 115% more likely to have a higher body weight compared to slower eaters.[75] One study in the United States found that women who ate more slowly consumed significantly less food yet felt fuller than those who ate quickly.[76] The study showed that:

- When eating quickly, the women consumed 646 calories in nine minutes

- When eating slowly, they consumed 579 calories in twenty-nine minutes

Over three meals per day, that would be a natural reduction of 200 calories. In addition, another study found that chewing more during mealtimes reduced snacking later in the day.[77] A further study found eating slower reduces BMI and waist circumference.[78]

Your feelings of hunger and fullness, and therefore your weight, are driven by hormones signalling to your brain. It is a complex system, which scientists continue to research in a bid to solve the problem of obesity. Essentially, your gut releases the 'hunger hormone' ghrelin, which tells your brain to eat, and the 'satiety hormone' leptin and other peptide hormones, such as cholecystokinin (CCK), peptide YY (PYY) and glucagon-like peptide-1 (GLP-1), which tell your brain you're full. It's believed that this process takes about twenty minutes and that when you eat quickly, your brain doesn't have enough time to receive those fullness signals.[79] Research shows that when you eat quickly, your gut decreases the release of the fullness hormones.[80] This suggests that if you eat more slowly, you will feel fuller, stop eating sooner and eat less.

Chewing your food longer can also increase the amount of nutrients you get out of it, which can keep you feeling full for longer.[81] The perfect number of chews often cited is thirty-two[82] but this can vary from ten to forty. Fibrous, chewy or crunchy foods, such as steak, cheese, fruits and nuts, require more chews per mouthful, while soft foods, such as fish or mashed banana, need fewer.[83]

Chewing your food thirty-two times all the time may feel laborious, but you can use the practice of eating slowly to appreciate your food. Enjoying your food rather than eating as fast as you can will change how you view it and reduce how much you eat. When you eat with others, use the NLP practice of modelling, by observing what the slowest eater does, and then the technique of pacing and leading, by matching your eating speed to theirs.

It is easy to overeat by about 100–200 calories a day without noticing – what Brian Wansink calls a 'mindless margin' in his book *Mindless Eating*.[84] He points out this equates to gaining ten extra pounds a year, and that even 10 calories a day would equate to one extra pound per year. This weight gain would be invisible but adds up to 10 pounds in a decade. When we examine how the average size of a dinner plate increased from 8.5–9 inches in the 1960s to

12 inches in 2009, we can easily see how we have learned to eat more.[85]

There is guidance on recommended portion size, but reducing your intake of food to that straight away could trigger a feeling of deprivation. Instead, you could gradually reduce your portion size. Wansink found that our brain does not notice a slight decrease and we can absorb a 20% reduction without feeling deprived.

In practice, that means if you usually have five spoons of ice cream, you'd now have four. You could decide to have four glasses of a fizzy drink a week instead of five, eight slices of bread instead of ten, sixteen chips instead of twenty, thirty-two crisps instead of forty.

You could play around with this comparative idea further. If you put your food on a smaller plate, you'd notice the 20% reduction even less. If you arrange your food as if you're on *MasterChef*, it will look more attractive. If you reduce the carbs by up to 20% and leave the vegetable and protein portions the same, the portion size will look similar while you are working your way to a more balanced plate.

It depends what you're eating in terms of what the 20% reduction would equate to in calories. If you are in the habit of eating a chocolate bar every day on your way home from work, and you eliminate one of the five bars in your work week, that could be

200–300 fewer calories a week and three to five fewer pounds a year.

This more conscious approach to eating helps you listen to your body and pay attention to your hunger levels. You learn to ask yourself what prompted the thought 'I'm hungry', consciously checking in with your body that it's actually hunger rather than the sight, idea or smell of a particular food that has triggered the thought, or that you really are hungry rather than thirsty.

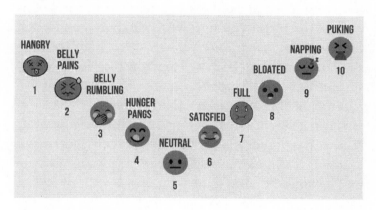

The Hunger Scale (adapted from the Advanced Diabetes Centre[86])

On the hunger scale, 5 is neutral, where you feel neither full nor hungry. When you start to feel hungry, you will get pangs at 4 and your stomach will be rumbling at 3. When you notice these signals, eat, because when you wait too long, you get over-hungry. If you're over-hungry, it is difficult to slow down your eating. You 'inhale' your food, trying to feel better and struggling to feel satiated as your brain does not get its full signal.

When you eat slowly, you will notice the food filling your stomach, and you can stop when you feel pleasantly full – not stuffed. A bit like when you are filling a saucepan with water – you don't fill it to overflowing.

A lifetime of mindless eating or encouragement to keep eating may have stopped you listening to your body's signals, or perhaps you learned to eat fast as a child to ensure you got your fair share or through FOMO. Growing up with plates piled high to show the luxury, amount and variety of the food – especially on Sundays and special occasions – accompanied with comments like 'Who wants this last piece?', 'Let's finish it up as there's no room in the fridge for leftovers', 'Go on, have some more, it won't hurt you' means you learned to overeat until you were physically in pain and collapsed on the sofa.

Eating slowly allows you to notice the changes in your body as you eat and recognise the signals you get when you start to feel full. It also allows you to enjoy your food. If that enjoyment is interrupted by negative thoughts, notice them, observe them, and then let them go. Rather than engage with them, waft them away.

As you build trust with your body, you learn that there is more than enough food to go around. You learn that it is OK to leave the rest of the food. At home, you can put it in the fridge. If you are in a restaurant, you can ask for a doggy bag. You also learn it is OK to finish after everyone else.

Make time to practise this new habit. Take your time and appreciate each mouthful and what it is giving your body rather than demolishing your smaller portion in seconds. That way, you'll feel satisfied, not deprived.

My story

I used to be so busy, I would put off eating or not even notice I was hungry. My focus and priority was always my work and I would often get to 7pm, still working, before I'd realise my stomach hurt and I felt sick from hunger.

I would then leave for home, an hour's drive, where my partner was cooking dinner. Unable to wait an hour, I would grab a pack of crisps and a flapjack, devour them as I drove, then eat a full meal when I got in.

I learned to prioritise me, to pay attention to and satisfy my hunger. I also chose to leave work earlier. I kept an emergency supply of nuts and seeds in my car so that I did not have to stop and grab something if I had left work later than intended or if I felt hunger pangs. In that way, I could satisfy them without overeating.

> ## CASE STUDY: Carole reduces her portion size
>
> A client, Carole, was not only a fast eater, but she ate everything she served up and even leftovers from others. She would, therefore, end up overeating, yet not feeling truly satisfied, and then the negative judgement would kick in as she put on weight.
>
> She decided she would try my trick, sitting on her hands between mouthfuls to help her eat more slowly and asking herself, 'Am I full yet?' as she ate. In addition, she challenged her habit of eating all the food she served by leaving something on her plate each mealtime. To address a previously unconscious value of not wasting food, she asked the others in the household to throw their leftovers straight in the bin. She chose the mantra 'It's OK to waste food' if she was tempted to finish everything on her plate.

SELF-COACHING ACTIVITY 32: Mindful eating

Try this mindful-eating exercise to retrain your brain. This opportunity to practise chewing more and slowly is often done as a five-minute meditation on a raisin.[87]

The steps are:

- Choose a small piece of food, either a food you enjoy and have put on your occasional eating list, or a food that you like the idea of and have decided to start eating.

- First, look at the food. Notice its size and shape, its texture, its colour.

- Next, smell the food. Is it a strong or mild smell? Sweet or sour? Does it bring back memories?
- Then, touch the food. Is it hard or soft? Moist or dry? Smooth, rough or sticky?
- Now take your first bite and chew *very slowly*. Notice the way it feels in your mouth, its flavour, any sound from the food itself or from the act of eating.
- Notice any feelings it triggers in you.
- Take about ten more chews to *very slowly* finish this first bite of food, noticing changes and sensations.
- When you've finished, take a second bite. Chew slowly, paying close attention to the flavour, changes in texture, the sensation of swallowing.
- Repeat for any further bites left.

Eat for a purpose

What if you chose your food for what it does for your wellbeing rather than to lose weight? Instead of a commercial diet that focuses on reducing calories or limiting the types of foods you eat, you could decide to concentrate on eating for you. Would you focus on heart, brain or gut health? Reducing your sugar levels? Feeling more energised?

Instead of taking foods out of your diet, you could start by adding foods in. You could choose food for what it gives you rather than eating what you think you *should* or *must* eat. Once you focus on eating for a purpose, eating consciously and aiming for balance in your diet, then you will make different choices.

I chose to prioritise food and lifestyle that improves mood and brain health. I found out I could boost my mood by feeding my happy chemicals or feel-good hormones through my diet and other lifestyle choices. The four primary neurotransmitters in this respect are dopamine, oxytocin, serotonin and endorphins.

When we feel low on energy and motivation, unable to focus and irritable, relying on caffeine, sugar or other stimulants to get us through the day, then chances are we're low on dopamine, the reward hormone. But you can eat foods that improve your dopamine levels. The dopamine diet, popularised by the chef Tom Kerridge, focuses on food built around tyrosine-rich ingredients. L-tyrosine is an amino acid used to produce the neurotransmitter dopamine, as you cannot get dopamine directly from food. The diet focuses on eating protein, such as lean and unprocessed meat like chicken; soy products; legumes like broad beans; high-protein dairy; eggs; omega-3-rich fish such as salmon; healthy fats like avocado; fruit like banana; nuts and seeds.[88] Adding the spice turmeric to your food as curcumin is known to boost brain function through the release of dopamine and serotonin.[89]

Succeeding at our goals and tasks releases dopamine. Completing exercise as part of our movement routine, including yoga and Pilates that are considered more for core strengthening and flexibility, boosts dopamine. Drinking green tea, which contains the amino acid L-theanine, is believed to improve mood, memory and metabolism.[90] This may further increase our dopamine by helping us achieve our weight-loss goal.

Reducing your stress levels will automatically boost your oxytocin, the cuddle hormone. You can also get a boost when you eat with someone else, and when you eat slowly and enjoy every mouthful. Playing relaxing music, doing yoga or meditating has been shown to release oxytocin, as has sex and other high-intensity exercise, so add these into your diet as your alternative activities or your reward![91] In terms of food, you can't get oxytocin directly, but you need magnesium for oxytocin to function properly. That means a diet packed with leafy green veg, avocados, bananas, nuts, seeds and legumes will have you feeling happier and less stressed.

Serotonin, the confidence hormone, is 95% produced in our gut, so focusing on gut health will boost our well-being.[92] Serotonin regulates metabolism and energy, affects memory function, sleeping patterns, and lifts our mood.[93] Tryptophan-rich foods, like poultry, tuna, milk and oats, provide the amino acid necessary for the body to produce serotonin.[94] It is worth noting that stress reduces our serotonin levels.[95] Interestingly, dark chocolate seems to be a great tool to help manage stress. It has been shown to inhibit cortisol and, as it contains some tryptophan, also helps boost serotonin.[96]

Endorphins, the euphoria hormones, reduce stress and help us power through challenging moments. Spicy foods and chilli peppers may boost endorphins, as does that chunk of high-quality dark chocolate. You could get a boost through social activities like laughter, group sport or dancing.[97]

One thing I chose to reduce was refined sugar as it has no nutritional benefits, adds unnecessary calories and causes inflammation. While the brain is dependent on glucose to function, I learned that too much can cause it to atrophy or shrink and is linked with dementia. Removing refined sugar changed my palate: anything sweetened had a 'metallic' taste and a raw carrot tasted sweet. I learned that vanilla is a great alternative solution as our brain has been trained to think it is sweet. I also trained myself to enjoy darker chocolate.

I chose to avoid low or reduced fat foods, as I learned that for everything the manufacturers take out, they put something in, which may well be sugar or chemicals. This felt odd, going against all the marketing and dieting programming I've been subjected to over the years, but I decided it's far better to have the natural full-fat version and reduce the amount I use because we need to eat fat. Fat is a source of energy and can keep us fuller longer, but the type of fat matters.[98] Foods with unsaturated fats provide essential fatty acids that the body cannot make itself, like Omega 3, which has vital health benefits. Salmon, seafood, avocado, olive oil, flaxseed and walnuts are foods that perform this function.[99]

Rather than follow eating rules that others have set, I came up with my own *Mindset Diet* rules:

- Instead of focusing on deprivation, calorie counting and losing weight, eat for a purpose, create a life I love and live it now – no putting stuff off until I have lost weight.

- Plan routines and create habits to support my wellbeing and stick to them each week.

- Focus on nutrition rather than calories; choose foods to help my brain and keep my gut healthy; try at least one new recipe each month.

- Eat with my body – not my mind or my emotions. Love and honour my body.

- Trust myself to eat what's right for me. Listen to and respect my gut as it is where my happy chemical serotonin is made.

- Accept that food is just food; good and bad are the labels society gives it. Let go of the judgements and decide instead to be neutral.

- Let go of guilt. Decide what I am going to eat, how much and when – for me.

- Decide what's important and set boundaries. Adhere to my values and decisions.

- Enjoy my food. Eat slowly, notice what it is giving me and be grateful for each mouthful.

- Have self-compassion because this is a life-long project, and we don't get things right the first time. This is the journey that creates lasting and sustainable change.

 SELF-COACHING ACTIVITY 33:
Your diet rules

Write your own diet rules: lifestyle, mindset and food. What will you focus on? What health outcome do you want? What is the difference that will make the difference to you? What would give you joy? How will you create balance?

Whatever rules you choose, make small changes at a time and ensure they feel right for you. Work towards achieving your rules rather than needing to be perfect now. Make up your rules by researching, observing your habits and listening to your body. If you decide to borrow from the principles of commercial diets, consider their benefits and drawbacks and decide what they could look like for you. Aim for balance.

Get wise to willpower

How often do you cite not having enough willpower as the reason you gave up on your diet? What is willpower? We're told we can lose weight if we have enough of it. We've been told that it's like a muscle, we need to build it, and that it's a finite resource we can run out of, and so we give up or give in.

Sometimes, lack of willpower is linked to decision fatigue, the idea that we are tired and have exhausted our capacity to make any more quality decisions that day. According to a study by Cornell University, we make 226.7 decisions a day about food.[100] Deciding whether to eat, what food to buy, what to cook, when to eat, where to eat, with whom to eat, how to eat, what not to eat...

No wonder food and eating are such driving forces in our lives. Our decisions are often made unconsciously, so influenced by our values and our beliefs, as covered in Chapter 3. This is why it's crucial our values and beliefs are in alignment with what we want to achieve.

Instant gratification theory explains why we fail to keep focused on our long-term goals and can be derailed by fulfilling an urge for pleasure or reward. Instant gratification is playing out when we justify doing something off plan. When we're saying, 'Who cares about the diet, this is too good to miss.' Triggers could be our environment, old habits, wanting to be spontaneous, lack of self-belief, hormones or mood.

Some common examples of instant gratification are:

- Eating the cake a coworker brings in as a reward or celebration for everyone

- Buying your favourite ice-cream because it's on special in the supermarket

- Hitting snooze on your alarm instead of getting up in time to make your breakfast and lunch

- Going out for dinner last minute instead of going home to eat your pre-prepared meal

- Feeling emotionally exhausted after a difficult day at work, so you order a takeaway or watch TV rather than going to your exercise class

- Staying up late to watch a film that looks interesting or is one you've been promising you'll watch for ages instead of getting a good night's sleep

- Craving and then eating something sweet

- Grazing on food left lying around

If you give in to instant gratification, you can end up laden with disappointment, guilt, shame or self-loathing. Then you either go on a crazy diet, desperate to lose 10 pounds by the weekend, or press the self-destruct button and eat, wondering how you ended up starting over yet again.

The antidote is delayed gratification, which is putting off that short-term gain because you have a bigger goal in sight. I learned it as a child when I had to make my Christmas goodies last for ages or save a portion of my pocket money rather than spending it on sweets or my favourite magazine.

If you didn't learn it as a child, here's how to retrain your brain:

- Make small changes. Put things off by ten minutes, then half an hour, several hours, a day. Keep building the delay factor.

- Find an alternative way to feed the feeling – distract yourself with mindful activities that absorb your attention instead.

- Decide on a mantra you will use when the desire strikes, for example 'maybe later'.

- Schedule in rewards so that you have them to look forward to – vary what your rewards are so that you learn other ways to feel good rather than by eating.

- Remember, the desire for instant gratification is only a thought – you don't have to act on it. You can change the story you tell yourself.

- When you know certain events trigger instant gratification for you, you can avoid them. Plan for events you can't avoid that you know will trigger your instant gratification.

The cure is not about building willpower, it's about developing self-awareness and self-compassion, focusing on what you really want and creating a plan to change. It's about having a clear vision of your future self and making decisions as your future self now. It's about examining your present strategies so you know in advance your triggers for temptation, what lines your inner voice feeds you to draw you in and what you are going to do to interrupt the pattern. What will you say to your inner voice? All these solutions are covered in this book, so you can take willpower out of the equation.

From an NLP perspective, when we apply Robert Dilts's Neurological Levels of Change model, which we looked at in Chapter 2, everything about us falls into alignment: our identity, our beliefs and values, the behaviours and skills we need to succeed and an awesome environment that supports our goal. Then we no longer need willpower as we have considered all aspects of our map of the world that are holding us back so that we can succeed. It's like we have found the tiny doll at the centre of a nesting Russian doll set, our core that drives us.

My story

I worked in an office where lots of my team were bakers, and the kettle was permanently surrounded by amazing cakes. At about 4pm, when I was tired and frustrated and still had several hours of work to do, I would go to make myself a cup of coffee. As I stood there waiting for the kettle to boil, I would think, 'That will make me feel better' and cut myself a piece of cake. Once in a while, that would be fine, but this was most days.

I decided to use the NLP Swish technique (see Self-coaching Activity 34) and change my self-talk to 'maybe later'. I didn't have a piece of any of those cakes again. In addition, I found that when I went out for coffee with friends, none of the cakes appealed to me. I thought they looked pretty and I would only have the coffee!

CASE STUDY: Sukhi's delay strategy

A client, Sukhi, really related to my 'maybe later' strategy as she felt it gave her choice. She used the phrase as a mantra whenever tempted to eat something as a reward when she got home from work. In conjunction with paying attention to her body's hunger signals rather than eating with her mind, this allowed her to reduce snacking without feeling deprived. Combining it with eating more slowly, Sukhi was able to create conscious eating habits.

SELF-COACHING ACTIVITY 34:
Swish technique

Study how you do the habit you want to change. Write down what you do, what you see as you do it, and notice your self-talk. Identify the trigger for the behaviour that you would like to change.

Close your eyes and bring to mind the picture of that moment when you do the habit. Put yourself in the picture, and then see it through your own eyes. Now set that picture aside for a moment.

Next, create in your mind a picture of yourself when you no longer have this issue. Put yourself in the picture and make it sharper or softer, brighter or more muted. Add any sound. Make it perfect for you. Then step out of the picture. Place the picture far out on the horizon where you can see yourself very small.

Bring back the old picture and put it on an imaginary plate of glass close to your face. Feel that old emotion flooding back. Connect that picture to the one on the horizon with an elastic band and twist the elastic band tighter and tighter and tighter. Let go so that the tiny picture on the horizon swishes at great speed and smashes through the old picture.

Notice how you feel differently, how you have more of the desired behaviour. Do this five more times, more quickly each time until you can no longer see or feel your old behaviour.

Imagine a time in the future when your old trigger happens and notice how you feel differently now.

CASE STUDY: Debbie quits sugar

A client, Debbie, couldn't resist sugar and she desperately wanted to change that. She believed she had no willpower around cakes, biscuits, anything sweet at all, and felt she had no off button.

We used the NLP Like to Dislike technique (Self-coaching Activity 35) to create an aversion to sugar. We exchanged how she thought about sweet foods with her thoughts and feelings about eating eels, a food that she absolutely detested and made her gag. This process changed her internal representation of all things sweet so much that she couldn't bear to go down the cake, sweet or biscuit aisles in the supermarket, it made her feel so ill.

SELF-COACHING ACTIVITY 35:
Like to Dislike technique

Decide what food you really like that you wish you didn't. Then decide on a food you hate so much, if you were to think of this instead when you considered the food you like that isn't serving you well, you would in no way want to eat it.

Picture that food you really love in your mind. Get a clear picture and notice where the image is, how big it is and what type of image. Notice the colours and textures, any smell, taste, feelings and reactions it creates, and where those feelings are.

Now do the same for the food you can't stand and want to change your like food to. Notice the differences between the two – for example, if the food you hate is a bigger and nearer picture, if it is black and white rather than colour, and if the smell clings to your nostrils and creates a burning sensation in your throat rather than excitement in your tummy.

Now picture the food you like and change the picture to be like the food you hate – in the case above, make it bigger and bring it nearer, make it black and white, make the smell cling to your nostrils and feel a burning sensation in your throat.

Imagine a time in the future when you try to eat the food you used to love so much and notice how you hate it now.

Summary

In this chapter, we have looked at building a lifestyle that is perfect for you, supports you to create your ideal eating plan and allows you to keep your weight off. You know what makes you feel good, and it is not following what has worked for other people. It is not overindulging yourself all the time.

When you make your eating more conscious, understand how eating for a purpose is different from dieting and deal with what is really undermining you rather than thinking that you don't have enough willpower, that is empowerment. Listening to the wisdom of your body, you will learn to trust yourself again, and from there you can gradually build the perfect diet for you.

People often cite a lack of willpower as being the reason they can't lose weight or keep the weight off when they have lost it, but in reality, it is not about building willpower. It's about developing self-awareness, building self-compassion, focusing on what we really want and creating a plan to change. We can then take willpower out of the equation.

In the next chapter, we will look at factors that may influence weight regain, how we may gradually go back to old habits and how to manage our mindset around special events.

EIGHT

Beware The Creep

One of the reasons going on a diet doesn't work is because it's not a long-term view, so we haven't planned what happens after the diet is done. We haven't adjusted our thinking and behaviours to match our new body shape; we still think the same as we always did.

How long does it take you to notice the weight creeping back on? Even with your well-formed outcome, there may be barriers you didn't notice at the time you formed it and old habits can return because you haven't fully understood what the habit was giving you.

When something happens to change our routine – a new job, a family emergency, a special occasion – it can be a struggle to keep to our new habits. We could find ourselves sliding back into old behaviours temporarily and if we don't pay attention, we forget to return to our new behaviours. Our putting it off until tomorrow thinking habit can leap back into action.

Understanding how specifically the body gains and loses weight is a relatively new field of research. What I have read suggests that reducing calories reduces our basal metabolic rate,[101] which is why we plateau when we lose weight and put it back on again. Also, a theory has been proposed that our body is programmed to regain weight.[102]

Reflecting on our progress and monitoring our habits are key to sustaining change over time. In this chapter, we look at ways to monitor your changes and manage special occasions so that you can avoid being caught out by the weight creeping back on.

Monitor for changes

Finding a way of monitoring yourself that is motivating and judgement free is crucial to avoid sabotage. Some people like to weigh themselves; others don't like to, but feel they should. Scales are loaded with judgement and can trigger disappointment, unhelpful beliefs and thoughts, and ultimately sabotage you and send you scurrying back to old habits. Just because of a tiny measure at a particular moment in time.

You probably don't weigh yourself at any time other than when you're on a diet, so it's become a system to find out if that deprivation and hell you've put yourself through is worth the effort. Perhaps you use it to check if you've put on weight because you ate a piece of cake this week. Perhaps it's something to avoid because it's associated with guilt when you know you haven't been 'good'.

Actually, you may have put on weight this week because your body was *due* to as part of your hormone cycle. Our body weight fluctuates in a cycle, so if you do want to weigh yourself, identify your personal pattern.[103] To do that, you'd need to weigh yourself every day for a month or maybe more without dieting to discover your natural weight range, then weigh yourself at the same point each month so that it is a real comparison. Even when you achieve the ideal body for you, you will fluctuate around that too. It doesn't mean you're putting on weight or you've been 'bad'.

What is important to notice is if you've gone back to old habits – those habits that caused you to gain weight. As it's your daily habits and triggers that are key to your success, you could keep a habit tracker so that you notice and act if you're starting to lose sight of the ones that make a difference. If you spot an old habit creeping back, use the secondary gain questions (Self-coaching Activity 27 in Chapter 5) to recognise what it gives you and work out how to achieve that in an alternative way.

Remember that your brain does not notice you increasing or decreasing your food intake by up to 20%,[104] so you are at risk of gradually overeating for your new body weight with its slowed metabolism. You may increase your portion size without noticing, add another spoonful to the pot as you're preparing the food. Perhaps you'll add an extra snack to your day or an extra glass of wine a week, a grabbed lunch because you are in a hurry. Those small additions will all make your weight creep up again and your shape change where your body most likes to add fat.

There are lots of ways to measure your success and monitor the changes you have made that do not require you to weigh yourself. You could measure:

- Your energy levels

- Your mood levels

- How comfortable your clothes are

- The fat around your middle – your waist-to-hip ratio

- The reduction in the medications you're taking

- How many times you honour you and say no

- How often you kept to your self-care plan

- Your food choices and amounts

The system you choose will depend on your goal and the small changes you decide to make. It depends on your why. It must be personal to you because it's *your* journey. What the scales tell you is only a tiny bit of information about your body health and your achievements, so why not ditch that old habit of weighing yourself and find a more rewarding way to measure your success and your progress on your journey of change.

My story

I had chosen not to weigh myself and instead decided to use an item of clothing to check what size I was. What I didn't do was schedule in my planner to try that item on, so I didn't notice the impact of the small changes – that I was gradually eating faster, my stress levels were increasing again, I was doing less of the cooking and shopping, so 'rarely' foods on my pyramid moved down to 'often' foods, one glass of wine became two. I dropped my walking habit due to the weather and didn't pick it up again, and we had an extraordinary number of special events in the space of a year.

On an unconscious level, I was aware of the changes, but I took no action to monitor or address them. I have now created a habit tracker in the back of my planner. I have accepted that my wellbeing is so important that I will monitor it for several years, if not always. Luckily, I love a list and ticking off the points on my list gives me a dopamine hit, so keeps me happy.

 SELF-COACHING ACTIVITY 36:
Monitor your progress and changes

Decide what you will measure to track your progress and monitor for creep. Make sure it is something that works for you, that you will stick to so that you don't gradually let things slide.

Enjoy special occasions

Do you love or loathe special occasions? Perhaps as a yo-yo dieter, you dreaded that big family or seasonal celebration – all those good intentions destroyed, and then having to start all over again afterwards. Perhaps you fought temptation because chocolate was everywhere, or felt guilty for having seconds and shame for eating the leftovers when you were already full. Perhaps you found yourself excusing an extra this and an extra that. You told yourself you could go back on your diet later.

Now you have shifted your mindset, you can listen to your body rather than eat with your mind. Once you reframe the occasion, you can enjoy it with ease and grace rather than guilt or stress.

The good news is fundamentally, traditional Christmas and Thanksgiving fare is nutritious and full of dopamine-rich foods. With that focus, you can ditch the guilt and instead enjoy what you choose to eat and drink, and do it mindfully. Appreciate the occasion. Be grateful for time with family and friends, and time with you.

Put in place a self-care plan so that you don't end up stressed. When you focus on your needs first, and then the needs of others, everything will fall into place. Design the perfect occasion for you and schedule activities on the calendar. Make the celebration more than just about food.

Apparently, most of us give ourselves permission to overeat or eat more when we're with others.[105] We may eat up to 48% more, so notice if you start negotiating with yourself. Eat slowly, enjoy the conversation, notice the sounds and smells. Listen to your body and make a loving choice for yourself.

Holidays may also be an excuse to blow out. Perhaps you would say to yourself, 'It doesn't matter, I'm on holiday,' or, 'I'll worry about it when I get back'. Perhaps you even used to go on a diet before and after your holiday.

With your new mindset, you can reframe that holiday as the perfect time to feel good and eat well, as is the summer season generally. The sun naturally makes us feel better and gives us energy and the confidence to make changes. You could choose to decide that a summer holiday gives you an incredibly convenient and easy way to exercise each day, or a time to float in the pool and dream and plan and be creative, or a chance to get some vitamin D to flood you with happy chemicals. A chance to eat nourishing fresh local food. That small shift in thinking will change your focus and your outcome.

If your first reaction to having indulged is to go on a diet, you may be interested to know that research suggests on average, people only put on about 3 pounds over the festive season or on holiday or a weekend away.[106] As it is mostly water retention rather than fat, it easily disappears when you go back to your usual lifestyle. It is only when you don't go back to your pre-occasion lifestyle that it becomes an issue.

If you feel a great desire to cleanse your body and lose those few pounds, why not reframe it as detox-ing your body? Not a detox diet. Our body doesn't require special diets or expensive supplements to eliminate toxins. It is naturally equipped to do so and has a sophisticated way that involves the liver, kidneys, digestive system, skin and lungs.[107] Going back to your awesome routine that keeps you feeling energised and well will allow you to return to your normal body weight.

Here are some examples of what your detox routine could include:

- Limit alcohol. Alcohol reduces the quality of your sleep, which impacts on your health, weight, energy, memory and productivity.

- Drink more water. Water regulates your body temperature, lubricates joints, aids digestion and nutrient absorption, and detoxifies your body by removing waste products.

- Reduce your intake of processed foods. These contain sugar, salt and unhealthy fats as well as chemicals, and lower your energy levels. The chemicals alone have been shown to cause weight gain.[108]

- Eat foods full of antioxidants as they can help your body fight oxidative stress. Examples of antioxidants include vitamin A, vitamin C, vitamin E, selenium, lycopene, lutein, beta-carotene and flavonoids. Prioritise the vegetables on your plate, eat berries or grapefruit for breakfast, snack on fruit, nuts or cacao, and drink green tea and coffee.

- Choose foods high in prebiotics, for example oats, bananas and garlic, and eat probiotics, such as yoghurt, miso and sourdough bread. Good gut health keeps your body's detox system working well, boosts your immune system and maintains your serotonin at high levels, which makes you feel so much better.

- Sleep. Getting enough sleep is paramount to supporting your body to maintain its immune system and remove toxins from your body.

- Get moving. Movement is great for reducing inflammation and supporting physical and mental wellbeing.

Maintaining your lifestyle and keeping your body how you want it is about reframing so that you can find balance and enjoy a normal way of living that is neither unhealthy nor deprivation.

Love your lifestyle

Does your present lifestyle bring you joy? Once you have designed the right lifestyle for you, you will feel more balanced and happier. When you have balance, you don't need willpower as you are never depriving yourself, just re-educating and re-training your brain. When you have balance, you feel less guilt as you don't overindulge yourself. You're not aiming to be perfect – just balanced. To achieve balance, you need to listen to your body, not your mind.

Use your anchor each day to maintain your vision of your future self. Without that motivation and the strong boundaries it upholds, you may find yourself creeping back to your old way of eating, especially if it was influenced by your friendship and family circle. Research has shown we are the average weight of the people we surround ourselves with, and their friends and their friends.[109] Like emotions, eating habits are contagious, so your perception of what is an acceptable body size and your behaviour changes according to your social network. The research found that a person's chances of becoming obese increase by 57% if a friend becomes obese, by 67% if a sister becomes obese and by 37% if a spouse becomes obese.

Lifestyle and environment are not the only influences on your body shape and weight. Science is working on understanding how the body regulates weight loss and weight gain.[110] It has proposed set point theory, the idea that we have a weight range that our body wants to stay in, and so our weight reverts there. Research suggests that if we lose more than 10% of our weight at one time, our body will fight to regain it.[111] It has also been proposed we have settling points that change as we put on weight. It is believed that this is a key reason people return to their pre-diet weight after a crash diet and that the only way to get it to decrease is through making long-term cognitive changes to counteract the setpoint mechanisms that are primed to drive weight gain.[112]

Further research theorises that we have a genetically influenced weight baseline set point.[113] As we continue to diet, we become hungrier, our metabolism slows, we begin to crave more food and our body gains back its weight.

Because the body understands dieting as starvation, it can adapt to burn fewer calories. The body's resting metabolic rate is capable of dropping between 50 and 700 calories for extended diets.[114] This research shows that the longer we diet, the more our metabolism slows. After the initial loss of water, then loss of some fat and muscle mass, our weight loss will slow, even if we eat the same number of calories, and we reach a plateau.

In response to the ineffectiveness of the traditional dieting-focused paradigm, a movement called Health at Every Size is growing.[115] It shifts the focus from weight management to health promotion – where weight loss may or may not be a side effect – and is emerging as standard practice in the eating disorders field. Here, there is concern about the damaging effects of the dieting paradigm as it contributes to an unhealthy food and body preoccupation, repeated cycles of weight loss and regain, distraction from other personal health goals, reduced self-esteem, and is associated with a culture of stigmatisation and discrimination.

Learning to eat less and differently and observing its impact, and then learning how to eat for our new body weight is a much better practice than continuous dieting. Sustainable eating practices keep our body in its most healthy state consistently, which is why visualising and creating a new lifestyle with foods and meals that we enjoy and will nourish us is so critical.

The 80/20 principle has been adopted in the weight-loss industry following nutritionist Teresa Cutter's *The 80-20 Diet Cookbook*.[116] The principle is that you spend 80% of the week eating healthy and nourishing food, what I refer to as 'always' and 'often' foods, and 20% of the week relaxing and socialising without guilt as you allow yourself to enjoy those 'sometimes' and 'occasional' foods. That 20% is 1.5 days where you can eat some foods that aren't in a core healthy diet. The principle is also used to guide the impact of what you eat compared to the impact of exercise on maintaining a healthy weight. This approach nourishes your body, keeps your energy balanced and creates a sustainable lifestyle even if it doesn't strictly adhere to the true Pareto Principle, first introduced by Italian economist Vilfredo Pareto in 1896, which stated that for many outcomes, roughly 80% of consequences come from 20% of causes.

Summary

One of the reasons going on a diet doesn't work is because it's not a long-term view and we haven't planned what happens after the diet is done. We haven't adjusted our thinking and behaviours to match our new body shape; we still think the same as we always thought.

Reflecting on our progress and monitoring our habits is key to sustaining change over time. That is what this chapter has been all about – looking at ways to monitor our changes and manage special occasions so that we can avoid being caught out.

Scales are loaded with judgement and can trigger disappointment, unhelpful beliefs and thoughts, and ultimately sabotage us. Even when we achieve the ideal body for us, our weight will fluctuate around that. It doesn't mean we're putting on weight or we've been bad. Rather than obsessing about weight, what is important to notice is if we've gone back to old habits.

Maintaining our lifestyle and keeping our body how we want it is about reframing so that we can find balance and enjoy a way of living that is neither unhealthy nor deprivation. We're not aiming to be perfect – just balanced. To achieve balance, we need to listen to our body, not our mind.

Remember, losing weight and keeping it off is a long game. It's letting go of those miracle promises to lose 20 pounds in 20 days, only to put them all back on, and instead creating a life for you that you love more than what you have now. Success takes time – time to change your thinking paradigm and your relationship with food.

Conclusion

Congratulations! You now understand environmental and internal influences on your eating and dieting habits in depth.

I hope the stories in the book have inspired you to change how you think about dieting. If you have done the activities, you will be well on your way to leaving behind the traps of yo-yo dieting and becoming an empowered eater. Because you now understand your eating patterns and triggered eating, you have far more options than those you were focusing on.

Society's advice for losing weight is to eat less and exercise more. You now understand how this advice is simplistic. It's not your fault that you have spent your life trying yet another miracle diet and joining yet another gym, only to struggle to lose any weight or be unable to maintain your weight loss.

With the information and practical activities I have shared with you in this book, you have tools and techniques to try a different approach. You will now be able to stop going on a diet and instead change your relationship with food so that you can halt the endless cycle of deprivation and disappointment.

I have provided you with insights and understandings to cut through the mental clutter you have built up over the years. I have shown you how to rewire your brain so your old thinking patterns no longer sabotage your efforts, how to update your beliefs and values from childhood so they don't hold you back, and how to develop self-compassion and an abundance mindset so you can transform your thinking. I wonder which change you will make first.

This book has provided you with a masterclass in what it really takes to lose weight for good, including rethinking your goal of losing weight and instead designing your future. You now have a clear path to a powerful, well-formed outcome that will help you focus on and achieve what really matters to you. You also have tools to build habits and routines that will help you thrive and propel you to your version of success, including in your professional world.

Remember, success isn't a straight line. It takes time, practice and patience to work your way through the stages of learning. As you apply what you have learned, revisit different chapters of the book and trust that you will get there. In difficult moments, remind yourself that everything passes. Your journey is about honouring you and focusing on your future self.

The knowledge and self-awareness you've gained from reading this book will enable you to find the joy in balanced and intuitive eating, no matter your weight. If you implement the ideas and write your own rules, you will transform your relationship with food and never be at the mercy of willpower again.

Will you feel even more supported to change if you use *The Mindset Diet* workbook? Download it here and start implementing the changes you want to make:

Will you feel even more empowered if you work with me one-to-one? You can change as quickly or as slowly as you want to. Consulting with me can speed up your change as we work through your patterns and resolve your questions as they present rather than as I've laid out in my book. For some people, it can be good to have a guide through the process of changing their thinking. Coaching was a powerful tool for me.

If you would like my help, then I would be delighted to provide that. As your conscience, your guide and your accountability with compassion, I will support you to have incredible lightbulb moments on your journey to more confidence and freedom from dieting. You can find out more at www.freetobenlp.co.uk.

You can join my Facebook Group at: www.facebook.com/groups/themindsetdiet and catch me on Instagram at: www.instagram.com/freetobenlp.

Notes

1   Allied Market Research, 'Weight loss and weight
    management diet market by product type: Global
    opportunity analysis and industry forecast, 2021–2027'
    (2021), www.alliedmarketresearch.com/weight-loss-
    management-diet-market, accessed September 2023
2   Fortune Business Insights, 'Anti-obesity drugs market size,
    share & COVID-19 impact analysis, by type (prescription
    drugs and OTC drugs), by distribution channel (hospital
    pharmacy and retail and online pharmacy), and regional
    forecast, 2023–2030' (2023), www.fortunebusinessinsights.
    com/anti-obesity-drugs-market-104783#, accessed
    3 October 2023
3   Z Briggs, 'Women spend an average of 17 years of their
    lifetime dieting', *Cosmopolitan* (19 September 2012), www.
    cosmopolitan.com/uk/body/health/a17370/women-diet-
    last-for-an-average-seventeen-years, accessed 3 November
    2023
4   G Pengelly, 'Cut the soaring cost of dieting down to
    size: Average woman spends £25,000 on weight plans
    in a lifetime – but getting trim needn't cost a fortune',

This Is Money (19 January 2014), www.thisismoney.co.uk/money/bills/article-2541757/Cut-soaring-cost-dieting-size-The-average-woman-spends-25-000-weight-plans-lifetime-getting-trim-neednt-cost-fortune.html, accessed 3 November 2023

5   R Stamp, 'Average person will try 126 fad diets in their lifetime, poll claims', *Independent* (8 January 2020), www.independent.co.uk/life-style/diet-weight-loss-food-unhealthy-eating-habits-a9274676.html, accessed 9 October 2023

6   B London, 'Over a decade of dieting: Women spend a staggering SEVENTEEN years of their lives trying to lose weight', *MailOnline* (18 September 2012), www.dailymail.co.uk/femail/article-2204944/Women-spend-staggering-SEVENTEEN-years-lives-trying-lose-weight.html, accessed 3 November 2023

7   D Kirkova, 'Five weeks of willpower: Most women give up diets after five weeks, two days and 43 minutes', *Daily Mail Online* (11 February 2013), www.dailymail.co.uk/femail/article-2276930/Five-weeks-willpower-Most-women-diets-weeks-days-43-minutes.html, accessed 6 November 2023

8   R Moss, 'Two thirds of Brits are on a diet "most of the time", study shows', *HUFFPOST* (10 March 2016), www.huffingtonpost.co.uk/2016/03/10/majority-brits-are-on-a-diet-most-of-the-time_n_9426086.html, accessed 3 October 2023

9   NHS Digital, 'Health Survey for England, 2021 part 1' (NHS, 2022), https://digital.nhs.uk/data-and-information/publications/statistical/health-survey-for-england/2021/part-2-overweight-and-obesity, accessed 3 October 2023

10   TH Chan, 'Obesity Prevention Source' (Harvard, 2023), www.hsph.harvard.edu/obesity-prevention-source/obesity-trends-original/obesity-rates-worldwide, accessed 3 October 2023

11   Department for Business and Trade, 'Food and Drink' (2023), www.great.gov.uk/international/content/investment/sectors/food-and-drink, accessed 3 October 2023

12   M Wait, 'The 3 day diet', *WebMD* (21 April 2023), www.webmd.com/diet/a-z/3-day-diet, accessed 3 November 2023

13   Centers for Disease Control and Prevention, 'Healthy
      weight, nutrition and physical activity' (2023), www.cdc.
      gov/healthyweight/losing_weight/index.html, accessed
      3 October 2023

14   D Ashtary-Larky et al, 'Effects of gradual weight loss
      v. rapid weight loss on body composition and RMR:
      A systematic review and meta-analysis', *British Journal of
      Nutrition*, 124/11 (2020), 1121–1132, https://pubmed.ncbi.
      nlm.nih.gov/32576318, accessed 3 November 2023

15   GR Hunter, EP Plaisance and G Fisher, 'Weight loss and
      bone mineral density', *Current Opinion in Endocrinology,
      Diabetes and Obesity*, 21/5 (2014), 358–362, www.ncbi.nlm.
      nih.gov/pmc/articles/PMC4217506, accessed 3 November
      2023

16   M Wdowik, 'The long, strange history of dieting fads', *The
      Conversation* (7 November 2017), https://theconversation.
      com/the-long-strange-history-of-dieting-fads-82294,
      accessed 3 October 2023

17   R Rosenthal, 'Commercial diets lack proof of their long-
      term success', *The New York Times* (24 November 1992),
      www.nytimes.com/1992/11/24/science/commercial-
      diets-lack-proof-of-their-long-term-success.html, accessed
      3 October 2023

18   T Kallmyer, '*Biggest Loser* then and now: Have former
      winners kept the weight off?', *Healthy Eater* (7 August
      2023), https://healthyeater.com/biggest-loser-then-now,
      accessed 3 October 2023

19   H Rosen, 'Is obesity a disease or a behavior abnormality?
      Did the AMA get it right?' (National Library of Medicine,
      2014), www.ncbi.nlm.nih.gov/pmc/articles/PMC6179496,
      accessed 9 October 2023

20   Harvard, 'Why people become overweight' (Harvard
      Medical School, June 2019), www.health.harvard.edu/
      staying-healthy/why-people-become-overweight,
      accessed 3 October 2023

21   T Coleman, 'Why diets don't work the second time' (Tara
      Coleman, no date), https://taracoleman.com/why-diets-
      dont-work-the-second-time, accessed 9 October 2023

22   MR Lowe et al, 'Dieting and restrained eating as
      prospective predictors of weight gain', *Frontiers in
      Psychology*, 4 (2013), www.frontiersin.org/articles/10.3389/
      fpsyg.2013.00577/full, accessed 6 November 2023

23 CN Ochner et al, 'Biological mechanisms that promote
    weight regain following weight loss in obese humans',
    Physiology & Behavior (2013), 106–113, www.ncbi.nlm.nih.
    gov/pmc/articles/PMC3797148, accessed 6 November
    2023

24 BIDMC Contributor, 'Week one: The science of set point'
    (Beth Israel Deaconess Medical Center, 2017), www.bidmc.
    org/about-bidmc/wellness-insights/nutrition/week-one-
    the-science-of-set-point, accessed 6 November 2023

25 Mayo Clinic Staff, 'Metabolism and weight loss: How you
    burn calories' (Mayo Clinic, 2022), www.mayoclinic.org/
    healthy-lifestyle/weight-loss/in-depth/metabolism/art-
    20046508, accessed 9 October 2023

26 F Spritzler, '6 mistakes that slow down your metabolism',
    Healthline (24 April 2019), www.healthline.com/
    nutrition/6-mistakes-that-slow-metabolism, accessed
    3 October 2023

27 M Thorpe, '10 solid reasons why yo-yo dieting is bad for
    you', Healthline (29 May 2017), www.healthline.com/
    nutrition/yo-yo-dieting, accessed 3 October 2023

28 R Dilts, *Changing Belief Systems with NLP* (Meta
    Publications, 1990)

29 K Haller, 'Branding: Why red and yellow is used by the
    fast-food industry (Karen Haller Behavioural Design
    Consultancy, no date), https://karenhaller.com/journal/
    branding-why-red-yellow-is-used-by-the-fast-food-
    industry, accessed 9 October 2023

30 Press Association, 'People who live or work near
    takeaways "are almost twice as likely to be obese"',
    The Guardian (14 March 2014), www.theguardian.com/
    society/2014/mar/14/takeaways-twice-likely-obese-study,
    accessed 3 October 2023

31 E Tolle, *The Power of Now: A guide to spiritual enlightenment*
    (Yellow Kite, 2001)

32 O Winfrey, 'What I know for sure', *O, The Oprah Magazine*
    (June 2008), www.oprah.com/omagazine/oprah-winfrey-
    on-body-image-what-i-know-for-sure-by-oprah, accessed
    9 October 2023

33 E Young, 'Lifting the lid on the unconscious', *New
    Scientist* (25 July 2018), www.newscientist.com/article/
    mg23931880-400-lifting-the-lid-on-the-unconscious,
    accessed 3 October 2023

34   K Spalding et al, 'Dynamics of hippocampal neurogenesis
      in adult humans', *Cell*, 153/6 (2015), 1219–1227, www.
      ncbi.nlm.nih.gov/pmc/articles/PMC4394608, accessed
      3 October 2023

35   KK Ganguly, 'Life of MK Gandhi: A message to youth
      of modern India', *Indian Journal of Medical Research*, 149
      (Supplement) (2019), S145–S151, www.ncbi.nlm.nih.gov,
      accessed 4 October 2023

36   K Neff, 'Self-compassion, instruments for researchers'
      (Center for Mindful Self-Compassion, 2023), https://self-
      compassion.org/self-compassion-scales-for-researchers,
      accessed 4 October 2023

37   K Neff, 'Self-compassion scale short form' (The University
      of Texas at Austin, 2011), https://self-compassion.org/
      wp-content/uploads/2021/03/SCS-SF-information.pdf,
      accessed 4 October 2023

38   A Craig, 'Discovery of "thought worms" opens window to
      the mind', *Queen's Gazette* (13 July 2020), www.queensu.ca/
      gazette/stories/discovery-thought-worms-opens-window-
      mind, accessed 5 October 2023

39   F Raes et al, 'Repetitive negative thinking outperforms
      loneliness and lack of social connectedness as a predictor
      of prospective depressive symptoms in adolescents',
      *Scandinavian Journal of Child and Adolescent Psychiatry and
      Psychology*, 3/8 (2020), 149–156, www.ncbi.nlm.nih.gov/
      pmc/articles/PMC7863726, accessed 5 October 2023

40   UC Davis Health, 'Gratitude is good medicine' (25
      November 2015)

41   *Marie Claire*, 'Kate Moss motto: 'Nothing tastes as good
      as being skinny feels', *Marie Claire Celebrity News* (16
      November 2009), www.marieclaire.co.uk/news/celebrity-
      news/kate-moss-motto-nothing-tastes-as-good-as-good-as-
      being-skinny-feels-175039, accessed 5 October 2023

42   VL Fulgoni et al, 'Avocado consumption is associated with
      better diet quality and nutrient intake, and lower metabolic
      syndrome risk in US adults: Results from the National
      Health and Nutrition Examination Survey (NHANES)
      2001–2008', *Nutrition Journal*, 12/1 (2013), www.ncbi.
      nlm.nih.gov/pmc/articles/PMC3545982, accessed
      5 October 2023

43   O Farr et al, 'Walnut consumption increases activation of
      the insula to highly desirable food cues: A randomized,
      double-blind, placebo-controlled, cross-over fMRI study',

Diabetes, Obesity and Metabolism, 20/1 (2017), 173–177, https://pubmed.ncbi.nlm.nih.gov/28715141, accessed 5 October 2023

44 Kaiser Permanente, 'Ask a doctor: Is juicing healthy?' (2023), https://healthy.kaiserpermanente.org/health-wellness/healtharticle.ask-a-doctor-is-juicing-healthy, accessed 9 October 2023

45 G Rubin, *Better Than Before: Mastering the habits of our everyday lives* (Two Roads, 2015)

46 D Erasmus, *Praise of Folly*, revised edition (Penguin, 1993)

47 J Clear, *Atomic Habits* (Penguin Random House, 2018)

48 S Covey, *The 7 Habits of Highly Effective People* (Simon & Schuster, 2013)

49 C Moore, 'What is negativity bias and how can it be overcome?', *Positive Psychology* (19 October 2019), https://positivepsychology.com/3-steps-negativity-bias, accessed 6 November 2023

50 N Stinson, 'Abundance mindset', *Chopra* (23 September 2019), https://chopra.com/articles/10-steps-to-develop-an-abundance-mindset, accessed 6 November 2023

51 Joe, 'Study focuses on strategies for achieving goals, resolutions', *Kitzu.org* (26 October 2021), https://kitzu.org/study-highlights-strategies-for-achieving-goals, accessed 3 November 2023

52 L Snopek et al, 'Contribution of red wine consumption to human health protection', *Molecules*, 23/7 (2018), 1684, www.ncbi.nlm.nih.gov/pmc/articles/PMC6099584, accessed 6 October 2023

53 Pull the Cork, 'Sugar in wine? Which wine has the lowest sugar content?' (2021), https://pullthecork.co.uk/which-wine-has-the-lowest-sugar-content, accessed 6 October 2023

54 J Huizen, 'Which type of alcohol has the fewest calories?', *Medical News Today* (21 July 2023), www.medicalnewstoday.com/articles/322568, accessed 3 November 2023

55 SE Swithers, 'Not-so-healthy sugar substitutes?', *Current Opinion in Behavioral Science*, 9 (2016), 106–116, www.ncbi.nlm.nih.gov/pmc/articles/PMC4846275, accessed 3 November 2023

56 DO Hebb, *The Organization of Behavior: A neuropsychological theory* (Wiley, 1949)

57 J Bolte Taylor, *Whole Brain Living: The anatomy of choice and the four characters that drive our life* (Hay House, 2021)

58 J Keller et al, 'Habit formation following routine-based versus time-based cue planning: A randomized controlled trial', *British Journal of Health Psychology*, 26/3 (2021), 807–824, https://bpspsychub.onlinelibrary.wiley.com/doi/full/10.1111/bjhp.12504, accessed 6 October 2023

59 CL Feingold and A Smiley, 'Healthy sleep every day keeps the doctor away', *International Journal of Environmental Research and Public Health*, 19/17 (2022), www.ncbi.nlm.nih.gov/pmc/articles/PMC9518120, accessed 6 October 2023

60 Kings College London, 'Sleep deprivation may cause people to eat more calories' (KCL, 2016), www.kcl.ac.uk/archive/news/kings/newsrecords/2016/11%20november-/sleep-deprivation-may-cause-people-to-eat-more-calories, accessed 6 October 2023

61 NF Watson et al, 'Recommended amount of sleep for a healthy adult: A joint consensus statement of the American Academy of Sleep Medicine and Sleep Research Society', *Sleep*, 38/6 (2015), 843–844, www.ncbi.nlm.nih.gov/pmc/articles/PMC4434546, accessed 10 October 2023

62 E John, 'Why exercise won't make you thin', *The Guardian* (19 Sept 2010), www.theguardian.com/lifeandstyle/2010/sep/19/exercise-dieting-public-health, accessed 6 October 2023

63 T Read, 'Walking 10 miles a day: How to get started and what to expect', *Healthline* (7 May 2023), www.healthline.com/nutrition/walking-10-miles-a-day, accessed 6 November 2023; M Winchell, 'Can running 4 times a week help me lose weight fast?', Livestrong.com (no date), www.livestrong.com/article/386849-can-running-4-times-a-week-help-me-lose-weight-fast, accessed 6 November 2023

64 G Joseph et al, 'A comparison of diet versus diet + exercise programs for health improvement in middle-aged overweight women', *Women's Health*, Jan–Dec (2020), www.ncbi.nlm.nih.gov/pmc/articles/PMC7325539, accessed 6 October 2023

65 S Makinde, 'Stress and weight gain without overeating' (Perfect Balance Clinic, 2020), www.perfectbalanceclinic.com/stress-and-weight-gain-without-overeating, accessed 6 November 2023

66 T Mann et al, 'Low calorie dieting increases cortisol', *Psychosomatic Medicine*, 72/4 (2010), 357–364, www.ncbi.nlm.nih.gov/pmc/articles/PMC2895000, accessed 6 October 2023

67   F Spritzler, '6 mistakes that slow down your metabolism',
      Healthline (24 April 2019), www.healthline.com/
      nutrition/6-mistakes-that-slow-metabolism#, accessed
      6 October 2023
68   UHN Staff, 'How much exercise is too much?',
      University Health News Daily (28 April 2020), https://
      universityhealthnews.com/daily/mobility-fitness/how-
      much-exercise-is-too-much, accessed 6 October 2023
69   A Chaix et al, 'When to eat: The importance of eating
      patterns in health and disease', *Journal of Biological Rhythms*,
      34/6 (2019), 579–581, www.ncbi.nlm.nih.gov/pmc/
      articles/PMC7213043, accessed 6 October 2023
70   E Koning and E Brietska, 'When you eat matters: How your
      eating rhythms impact your mental health', *Queen's Gazette*
      (17 March 2022), www.queensu.ca/gazette/stories/when-
      you-eat-matters-how-your-eating-rhythms-impact-your-
      mental-health, accessed 6 October 2023
71   K Sampson, 'Late-night eating and weight gain', *The
      Harvard Gazette* (4 October 2022), https://news.harvard.
      edu/gazette/story/2022/10/study-looks-at-why-late-
      night-eating-increases-obesity-risk, accessed 9 October 2023
72   K Sampson, 'Late-night eating impact' (Harvard Medical
      School, 2022), https://hms.harvard.edu/news/late-night-
      eating-impact, accessed 8 October 2023
73   KG Baron et al, 'Contribution of evening macronutrient
      intake to total caloric intake and body mass index', *Appetite*,
      60/1 (2013), 246–251, https://pubmed.ncbi.nlm.nih.
      gov/23036285, accessed 8 October 2023
74   GA O'Reilly et al, 'Mindfulness-based interventions for
      obesity-related eating behaviors: A literature review',
      Obesity Review, 15/6 (2015), 453–461, www.ncbi.nlm.nih.
      gov/pmc/articles/PMC4046117, accessed 8 October 2023
75   C Madden et al, 'Faster self-reported speed of eating is
      related to higher body mass index in a nationwide survey
      of middle-aged women', *Journal of the American Dietetic
      Association*, 111/8 (2011), 1192–1197, https://pubmed.ncbi.
      nlm.nih.gov/21802566, accessed 5 October 2023
76   University of Rhode Island, 'URI study confirms popular
      dietary lore: Eating slowly really does inhibit appetite',
      Rhody Today (15 November 2006), www.uri.edu/
      news/2006/11/uri-study-confirms-popular-dietary-
      lore-eating-slowly-really-does-inhibit-appetite, accessed
      5 October 2023

77 S Higgs and A Jones, 'Prolonged chewing at lunch
    decreases later snack intake', *Appetite*, 62 (2013), 91–
    95, www.sciencedirect.com/science/article/abs/pii/
    S0195666312004710?via%3Dihub, accessed 6 November 2023

78 Y Hurst and H Fukuda, 'Effects of changes in eating speed
    on obesity in patients with diabetes: A secondary analysis
    of longitudinal health check-up data', *BMJ Open* (2018),
    https://bmjopen.bmj.com/content/8/1/e019589, accessed
    6 November 2023

79 AY Yeung and P Tadi, 'Physiology, obesity neurohormonal
    appetite and satiety control', *StatPearls* (2023), www.ncbi.
    nlm.nih.gov/books/NBK555906, accessed 6 November 2023

80 A Kokkinos et al, 'Eating slowly increases the postprandial
    response of the anorexigenic gut hormones, peptide
    YY and glucagon-like peptide-1', *The Journal of Clinical
    Endocrinology & Metabolism*, 95/1 (2010), 333–337, https://
    academic.oup.com/jcem/article/95/1/333/2835331,
    accessed 6 November 2023

81 BA Cassady et al, 'Mastication of almonds: effects of lipid
    bioaccessibility, appetite, and hormone response', *The
    American Journal of Clinical Nutrition*, 89/3 (2009), 794–800,
    https://www.sciencedirect.com/science/article/pii/
    S0002916523237508, accessed 6 November 2023

82 E Cirino, 'Chewing your food: Is 32 really the magic
    number?', *Healthline* (20 March 2020), www.healthline.
    com/health/how-many-times-should-you-chew-your-
    food, accessed 9 October 2023

83 NHS, *Patient Information Factsheet: Level 7 diet (easy to chew)*
    (University Hospital Southampton NHS Foundation
    Trust, 2020), www.uhs.nhs.uk/Media/UHS-website-2019/
    Patientinformation/Medicinestherapiesandanaesthetics/
    Level-7-diet-easy-to-chew-2445-PIL.pdf, accessed 6
    November 2023

84 B Wansink, *Mindless Eating: Why we eat more than we think*
    (Bantam Books, 2006)

85 S Frank, 'The history of dinner plate sizes corresponds to
    the increase in obesity', *Blog Spot* (18 August 2019), http://
    foodandarts.blogspot.com/2011/05/history-of-plate-sizes.
    html, accessed 5 October 2023

86 Advanced Diabetes Centre, 'Hunger Scale – Coping with
    your hunger pangs' (2016), http://advanceddiabetescentre.
    com/blog/hunger-scale-coping-with-your-hunger-pangs,
    accessed 8 October 2023

87   JB Nelson, 'Mindful eating: The art of presence while you eat', *Diabetes Spectrum*, 30/3 (2017), 171–174, www.ncbi.nlm.nih.gov/pmc/articles/PMC5556586, accessed 6 November

88   A McCabe, 'Dopamine: How what we eat impacts our brain chemistry', *Nutritionist Resource* (7 April 2021), www.nutritionist-resource.org.uk/memberarticles/dopamine-how-what-we-eat-impacts-our-brain-chemistry, accessed 6 November 2023

89   SK Kulkarni and A Dhir, 'An overview of curcumin in neurological disorders', *Indian Journal of Pharmaceutical Sciences*, 72/2 (2010), 149–154, www.ncbi.nlm.nih.gov/pmc/articles/PMC2929771, accessed 9 October 2023

90   L Ming-Yue et al, 'L-theanine: A unique functional amino acid in tea (*Camellia sinensis* l.) with multiple health benefits and food applications', *Frontiers in Nutrition*, 9 (2022), www.ncbi.nlm.nih.gov/pmc/articles/PMC9014247, accessed 6 November 2023

91   Amen Clinics, 'Oxytocin: 13 natural ways to increase the love hormone' (2022), www.amenclinics.com/blog/oxytocin-13-natural-ways-to-increase-the-love-hormone, accessed 6 November 2023

92   J Appleton, 'The gut-brain axis: Influence of microbiota on mood and mental health', *Integrative Medicine*, 17/4 (2018), 28–32, www.ncbi.nlm.nih.gov/pmc/articles/PMC6469458, accessed 6 November 2023

93   JM Yabut et al, 'Emerging roles for serotonin in regulating metabolism: New implications for an ancient molecule', *Endocrine Reviews*, 40/4 (2019), 1092–1107, https://academic.oup.com/edrv/article/40/4/1092/5406261, accessed 6 November 2023

94   DM Richard et al, 'L-tryptophan: Basic metabolic functions, behavioral research and therapeutic indications', *International Journal of Tryptophan Research*, 2 (2009), 45–60, www.ncbi.nlm.nih.gov/pmc/articles/PMC2908021, accessed 6 November 2023

95   R Natarajan et al, 'Chronic-stress-induced behavioral changes associated with subregion-selective serotonin cell death in the dorsal raphe', *Journal of Neuroscience*, 37/26 (2017), 6214–6223, www.jneurosci.org/content/37/26/6214, accessed 6 November 2023

96   PH Wirtz et al, 'Dark chocolate intake buffers stress reactivity in humans', *Journal of the American College of*

Cardiology, 63/21 (2014), 2297–2299, www.sciencedirect. com/science/article/pii/S0735109714015836, accessed 6 November 2023

97 EEA Cohen et al, 'Rowers' high: Behavioural synchrony is correlated with elevated pain thresholds', *Biology Letters*, 6/1 (2010), 106–108, https://pubmed.ncbi.nlm.nih. gov/19755532, accessed 6 November 2023

98 RA Samra, 'Fats and satiety'. In: Montmayeur JP and le Coutre J (eds), *Fat Detection: Taste, texture, and post ingestive effects* (CRC Press/Taylor & Francis, 2010), Chapter 15. Available from: www.ncbi.nlm.nih.gov/books/NBK53550, accessed 6 November 2023

99 Harvard TH Chan School of Public Health, 'Omega-3 fatty acids: An essential contribution' (Harvard School of Public Health, no date), www.hsph.harvard.edu/nutritionsource/ what-should-you-eat/fats-and-cholesterol/types-of-fat/ omega-3-fats, accessed 6 November 2023

100 B Wansink and J Sobal, 'Mindless eating: The 200 daily food decisions we overlook', *Environment and Behavior*, 39/1 (2007), 106–123, https://journals.sagepub.com/ doi/10.1177/0013916506295573, accessed 6 November 2023

101 PA Molé, 'Impact of energy intake and exercise on resting metabolic rate' (National Library of Medicine, 1990), https://pubmed.ncbi.nlm.nih.gov/2204100e, accessed 10 October 2023

102 Diabetes & Endocrinology, 'Why people diet, lose weight and gain it all back' (Cleveland Clinic Health Essentials, 2019), https://health.clevelandclinic.org/why-people-diet-lose-weight-and-gain-it-all-back, accessed 10 October 2023

103 C Jackle, 'Why does my weight fluctuate? Pt 1: Menstrual cycle' (Xplore Nutrition, 2018), www.xplorenutrition.com/ blog/2018/02/08/weight-fluctuate-pt-1-menstruation, accessed 6 November 2023

104 B Wansink and J Sobal, 'Mindless eating: The 200 daily food decisions we overlook', *Environment and Behavior*, 39/1 (2007), 106–123, https://journals.sagepub.com/ doi/10.1177/0013916506295573, accessed 6 November 2023

105 University of Birmingham, 'People eat more when dining with friends and family – study' (4 October 2019), www. birmingham.ac.uk/news-archive/2019/people-eat-more-when-dining-with-friends-and-family-study, accessed 5 October 2023

106   M Chalabi, 'How much weight will I gain at Christmas and
      how long will it take to lose it?', *The Guardian* (20 December
      2013), www.theguardian.com/news/reality-check/2013/
      dec/20/how-much-weight-will-i-gain-at-christmas-and-
      how-long-will-it-take-to-lose-it, accessed 5 October 2023

107   K Miller, 'How to naturally detox your body', *Health*
      (28 November 2023), www.health.com/weight-loss/how-
      to-detox, accessed 19 December 2023

108   BBC News, 'How harmful can ultra-processed foods
      be for us?', video (10 June 2023), www.youtube.com/
      watch?v=wIhbYA5QLEw, accessed 5 October 2023

109   NA Christakis et al, 'The spread of obesity in a large social
      network over 32 years', *New England Journal of Medicine*,
      357 (2007), 370–379, www.nejm.org/doi/full/10.1056/
      NEJMsa066082, accessed 5 October 2023

110   A Bosy-Westphal et al, 'Is there evidence for a set point
      that regulates human body weight?', *F1000 Medicine
      Reports*, 2/59 (2010), www.ncbi.nlm.nih.gov/pmc/articles/
      PMC2990627, accessed 5 October 2023

111   BIDMC Contributor, 'Week one: The science of set point'
      (Beth Israel Deaconess Medical Center, Oct 2017), www.
      bidmc.org/about-bidmc/wellness-insights/nutrition/
      week-one-the-science-of-set-point, accessed October 2023

112   VM Ganipisetti and P Bollimunta, 'Obesity and set-point
      theory,' *StatPearls* (Jan 2023), www.ncbi.nlm.nih.gov/
      books/NBK592402, accessed 6 November 2023

113   M Renkl, 'Destined to inherit your mom's body', *NBC News*
      (8 February 2010), www.nbcnews.com/id/wbna35254750,
      accessed 5 October 2023

114   L Carroll, 'How metabolism slows down when you try to lose
      weight', *NBC News* (27 January 2022), www.nbcnews.com/
      health/health-news/study-shows-metabolism-slows-weight-
      loss-causing-diets-fail-rcna13543, accessed 5 October 2023

115   L Bacon et al, 'Weight science: Evaluating the evidence
      for a paradigm shift', *BMC Nutrition Journal*, 10/9
      (2011), https://nutritionj.biomedcentral.com/
      articles/10.1186/1475-2891-10-9, accessed 5 October 2023

116   T Cutter, *The 80–20 Diet: 12 weeks to a better body* (Murdoch
      Books, 2016)

Acknowledgements

This book was made possible through the belief, encouragement and help of many others.

First, I'd like to thank my clients who have trusted me to support their wellbeing, change their relationship with food or build their confidence and self-belief so they could make different choices. Thank you for allowing me to share elements of your stories to enrich the reader experience. Your faith in me and your feedback gave me the confidence that I could write this book.

Massive thanks to my beta readers for their feedback and help shaping the book into its final version: Kate McCartney, an incredible NLP master trainer, coach and author; Kylie Combellack, an astute student and teacher; and especially Jane Aronovitch, a friend, colleague and editor of many years who also helped advise with the book structure.

To the Rethink Press team who have spun their magic and elevated my draft to this final product. In particular, deep gratitude to Lucy McCarraher who encouraged, mentored and supported me and other women writers to get their book out into the world through her *A Book of One's Own* programme. Thank you also to all the women in the group who shared their experiences and encouraged us all to keep going.

Thank you to master NLP trainers Toby and Kate McCartney for their awesome courses that changed my life and opened a new way of thinking and understanding of the world and myself. You model using business to make a difference in the world and go above and beyond, supporting, encouraging and celebrating those who pass through your programmes so that they too use the skills you teach to go out and make a difference.

Thanks to Sue Williams for giving me that first taste of being published in a chapter of her book *Believe You Can Live a Life You Love at 50+* and to Rosemary Cunningham for suggesting my name to Sue.

Thanks to Angela Roth, a former diet programme coach, who encouraged me and helped me believe that my message matters.

Finally, thank you to my partner Andrew Bovingdon for his unwavering belief in me and for not allowing me to give up on my book.

The Author

Caroline Tyrwhitt is an NLP trainer and a Personal Care Institute accredited health and wellbeing coach. She has a great passion for education, words and women's empowerment, and this has been reflected in her career – from the banking industry in the 1980s, working as a technical editor in Toronto, doing degrees in linguistics and education as a mature student, to a twenty-five-year career in the education sector, through to her current work with women and their relationship with food.

Caroline was regularly on a diet. This wasn't a problem to her until she hit her forties and was working as a leader in education. At that point, work overwhelm, unregistered impacts of ageing and her daily habits caused her to steadily gain weight, and she had neither energy nor motivation to go on a diet again.

It was when she started to study NLP that Caroline changed her relationship with food. NLP was a game changer for her. She undid her food programming – those triggers, habits and self-talk that led to her losing weight and gaining it back – as well as uncovering the one key that unlocked the ease and flow in weight loss for her.

From her own experience, from research and from helping other women, she learned that losing weight is complex, not least because our bodies are not designed to do so. We unravel one aspect that's holding us back and feel great for a while, only to then discover another layer that needs tackling. When she applied the tools to help her and other women lose weight, she discovered those same shifts also helped boost confidence, which then impacted in the business world. The process she has followed has helped her develop more self-compassion and self-acceptance, which she brings to her way of working and helps other women to develop too.

Caroline has struggled with the idea of working in the weight-loss industry as it has such negative connotations for her. She prefers instead to focus on wellbeing and self-empowerment, helping women make small changes that develop a sustainable lifestyle bespoke to them. She aims to support women to feel truly happy, because it's not enough to lose weight to achieve an image or body that other people tell them they should have.

⊕ www.freetobenlp.co.uk/meet-caroline

in www.linkedin.com/in/
caroline-tyrwhitt-mindset-coach

f www.facebook.com/carotyr